Important Words
A Book for Poets and Writers

Bill Brown
Hume-Fogg Academic High School
Nashville, Tennessee

and

Malcolm Glass
Austin Peay State University
Clarksville, Tennessee

With a Foreword by William Stafford

BOYNTON / COOK PUBLISHERS
HEINEMANN
Portsmouth, NH

BOYNTON/COOK PUBLISHERS, INC.
A Subsidiary of
HEINEMANN EDUCATIONAL BOOKS, INC.
361 Hanover Street, Portsmouth, NH 03801
Offices and agents throughout the world

Every effort has been made to contact students and copyright holders for permission
to reprint borrowed material. We regret any oversights that may have occurred and
would be happy to rectify them in future printings of this work.

Acknowledgments begin on page xi.

Photography credits:
Dan Gair: 82, 150
Malcolm Glass: 94
Gary Langley: 124
Frank O'Brien: 12, 34
J. Michael Rogers: xxvi, 24, 108
Peter Stillman: 56

Library of Congress Cataloging-in-Publication Data
Brown, Bill, 1948 Sept. 17-
    Important words : a book for poets and writers / Bill Brown and
Malcolm Glass ; with a foreword by William Stafford.
        p.   cm.
    Includes index.
    ISBN 0-86709-271-8
    1. English language—Composition and exercises—Study and teaching
(Secondary) 2. Poetry—Study and teaching (Secondary) 3. Creative
writing (Secondary education) I. Glass, Malcolm. II. Title.
LB1631.B768   1991
808'.042'0712—dc20   91-122
                                                          CIP

Designed by Hunter Graphics.
Cover photo by J. Michael Rogers.
Printed in the United States of America.
91 92 93 94 95   9 8 7 6 5 4 3 2 1

Contents

An Invitation

Sometimes a book will help you pick up your life and carry it along in a new way. This book, aimed at student writers, could do that. It upends many ideas you might expect:

- As you write, don't think about spelling, punctuation, or neatness.
- Anyone can write.
- It is perfectly all right to fail.
- Your so-called failures may sometimes teach you more than your successes.
- If you get stuck, reread: your own words will get you started again.

This book takes you from right where you are and accompanies you on a step-by-step discovery: "A writer's most important job is to find (not invent, but discover through the process of writing) how and why a subject matters."

Students and teachers, writing together, go on this journey of self-discovery, and the authors plunge in themselves; they are direct in speaking from their own lives and efforts.

And you don't wait in this book; you don't juggle forms and techniques in getting ready to write from the self about things closest to you. Those forms and techniques come later, as they suggest themselves and take their place in relation to important material that springs from the momentum of writing.

It's a whole rich world out there, for students, for teachers.

You're invited.

William Stafford

Preface

Our editors suggested that we write a preface to this book to tell readers why we wrote it. There couldn't be an easier task: we wrote this book because the theories and practices we present here *work*. Time and time again these assignments have led writers to create excellent poetry and prose. Many of the pieces we offer as examples, written in our classes and workshops, have won national awards, and their authors are continuing to write and to be published in respectable journals.

We have worked with writers of all ages: with beginners and more accomplished and published writers, with student writers, teacher writers, writers no longer in school. Their work is consistently good, sometimes astonishingly complex and subtle. Why? We believe the success of this program of assignments lies in these principles:

- Almost everything in this book, from its basic principles to its specific assignments, grew out of our experiences as writers and our familiarity with the ways writers work, with their subjects and their ways of handling them.

- Humans learn performance skills by imitation and emulation. This is true of virtually all writing, but it is especially true of creative writing. Writing, like any performance skill, requires a great deal of self-confidence, and emulation seems to bolster it. The writer senses, "I can do that, and maybe do it even better." Sometimes trying to emulate a poet as famous and skilled as Richard Wilbur may be a bit intimidating, but don't let your respect for a writer or his work keep you from trying.

- The assignments in this book, then, are based on the principle of modeling: we present pieces of writing that suggest subjects and ways to write about them. Many are written by students who may have been writing only a short time; some are by us; others are by poets who have published so widely that you may recognize their names. As far as we are concerned, a poem is a poem; and the age or experience of the writer often has little to do with its value as a piece of writing or as a stimulus to get writers started on their own poems. Although some of the poems are noticeably better than others, we think you will respond easily and strongly to almost all of them.

- It has become a commonplace perception that one can write about absolutely anything, even something as insignificant as a disposable razor. This may be theoretically true, but it is not a directly useful premise for most beginning writers. A writer's most important job is to find (not invent, but discover through the process of writing) how and why a subject matters to the writer. If a writer doesn't care about the subject or what the writer is saying, the writing will indeed be *care-less*. Subject matter *does* matter. As Robert Frost said in his essay, "The Figure a Poem Makes": "The object in writing poetry is to make all poems sound as different as possible from each other, and the resources for that of . . . words, sentences, meter are not enough. We need the help of context—meaning—subject matter. That is the greatest help towards variety."

- The subjects closest to the writer are most likely to be the best material for writing. They are uniquely the writer's own, and he or she cares about them. The best poems teach the heart, and to do that they must come from the heart. And they must be spoken from the heart in the writer's natural and honest voice.

At the beginning of this preface we spoke of the book as "a program of assignments." There is a design, an order, and rationale to this book. Don't feel that you must write every single assignment in a chapter but try to do as many as you can. You may respond to some assignments with a mediocre piece of writing, or worse. Don't worry if that happens; it is perfectly all right to fail. Writing is learned by trial and error; your so-called failures may sometimes teach you more than your successes. If a particular assignment doesn't appeal to you, skip over to a poem or writing idea that does. While you should feel free to pick and choose assignments in any chapter, it is important to follow the chapters in order since they present subjects and techniques in an order of increasing complexity.

This book also has the shape and movement of a poem. It will take you on a journey that parallels the pattern of your life. You will begin with the most important subject, with something you care about most—yourself. From that beginning you will move out into the world, ranging farther and farther away and returning to the self from time to time so you won't lose sight of your unique and personal perspective. In the last few chapters you will venture from your past experience and present observation into the lives of other people, other creatures, and into the future, into worlds that exist only in your imagination.

Along the way, you will find you are also on a journey that will take you from writing intuitively and instinctively to writing with a greater understanding of the techniques available to you. This book is, then, a journey from freedom to self-discipline.

PS As you read this book, you may wonder who wrote which chapter or section. The truth is we both had a hand in writing and rewriting nearly everything. If you can't tell whose words are whose, we'll be pleased: This has been a happy collaboration, and we want to be known as a team speaking in the first-person singular.

Acknowledgments

We are grateful to the publishers and individuals below for granting permission to reprint material from previously published works.

Chapter 1

Pages 1-2: "A Change of Hands" by Bill Brown. First published in *Number One*. Reprinted by permission.

Page 3: "Epiphany" by Stephanie Johnston from *Scholastic Scope* (May 1986) and *Literary Cavalcade* (February 1987). Reprinted by permission of Scholastic, Inc., and the author.

Pages 6-8: "The Coming of Winter" by Amy Evans from *Scholastic Scope* (May 1986). Reprinted by permission of Scholastic, Inc., and the author.

Pages 8-9: "November Rain" by Amy Evans from *Literary Cavalcade* (May 1986). Reprinted by permission of Scholastic, Inc., and the author.

Pages 9-10: "Marin-An" by Gary Snyder: *The Back Country*. Copyright © 1968 by Gary Snyder. Reprinted by permission of New Directions Publishing Corporation.

Chapter 2

Page 13: "In the Australian Oak" from *Bone Love* by Malcolm Glass, 1979. Orlando: University of Central Florida Press. Reprinted by permission.

Page 14: "Fright" by Wendolyn Bozarth from *Scholastic Scope* (May 1986). Reprinted by permission of Scholastic, Inc., and the author.

Page 15: "Pulled Out of Bed" by Tracey Tomlinson from *Literary Cavalcade* (May 1986). (First published as "Silent Hands.") Reprinted by permission of Scholastic, Inc., and the author.

Page 16: "Root Cellar," copyright 1943 by Modern Poetry Association, Inc. From *The Collected Poems of Theodore Roethke* by Theodore Roethke. Used by permission of Doubleday, a division of Bantam, Doubleday, Dell Publishing Group, Inc.

Pages 16-17: "Lost Treasure" from *In the Shadow of the Gourd* by Malcolm Glass, 1990. St. Paul, MN: New Rivers Press. Reprinted by permission.

Page 18: "Clayton Bloom Came Mornings" from *Gilead: Notes on a Catskill Hamlet* by Peter Stillman, 1986. Roxbury, NY: The Roxbury Arts Group. Reprinted by permission.

Page 20: "George's Place" from *Gilead: Notes on a Catskill Hamlet* by Peter Stillman, 1986. Roxbury, NY: The Roxbury Arts Group. Reprinted by permission.

Chapter 3

Page 27: "Yearbook" by Sister Mary Lucina. First published in *Visions—International*. Reprinted by permission.

Pages 27-28: "Upon Finding a Photo of My Second Grade Class" by Jill P. Baumgaertner. First published in *Visions—International*. Reprinted by permission.

Page 29: "Gar" from *In the Shadow of the Gourd* by Malcolm Glass, 1990. St. Paul, MN: New Rivers Press. Reprinted by permission.

Chapter 4

Page 36: "That Morning" by Bill Brown. First published in *Hogshead Review*. Reprinted by permission.

Pages 37-38: "The Writer" from *The Mind-Reader: New Poems,* copyright © 1971 by Richard Wilbur, reprinted by permission of Harcourt Brace Jovanovich, Inc.

Page 38: "White Skies" by Barry Gilmore from *Scholastic Scope* (May 1987). Reprinted by permission of Scholastic, Inc., and the author.

Page 39: "Spider" by Scholle Sawyer from *Literary Cavalcade* (1988). Reprinted by permission of Scholastic, Inc., and the author.

Pages 40-41: "Family Reunion" by Eleanor Womack. First published in *Old Hickory Review*. Reprinted by permission.

Page 42: "This Is Just to Say." William Carlos Williams: *Collected Poems, Vol. 1 1909-1939*. Copyright 1938 by New Directions Publishing Corporation. Reprinted by permission of New Directions Publishing Corporation.

Page 43: "Less Than an Apple" by Bill Brown. First published in *Visions—International*. Reprinted by permission.

Page 48: "Eulogy for My Father" by Tiffany Thurman. First published in *Old Hickory Review*. Reprinted by permission.

Page 50: "April Fool" from *Holding On By Letting Go* by Bill Brown, 1986. Flatwoods, TN: Bucksnort Press. Reprinted by permission.

Pages 54-55: "Silent Hope" by Bill Brown. First published in *Old Hickory Review*. Reprinted by permission.

Chapter 5

Page 58: "How It Began" from *A Glass Face in the Rain* by William Stafford. Copyright © 1982 by William Stafford. Reprinted by permission of Harper & Row Publishers, Inc.

Page 59: "Blues for Old Dogs" by Paul Zimmer from *The American Zimmer*, 1984. Athens, GA: The Press of the Nightowl. Reprinted by permission.

Pages 59-60: "The Hermit Meets the Skunk," *Our Ground Time Here Will Be Brief* by Maxine Kumin. Copyright © 1972 by Maxine Kumin. All rights reserved. Reprinted by permission of Viking Penguin, a division of Penguin Books USA, Inc.

Page 61: "The Crows" by Leah Bodine Drake from *Hawk and Whippoorwill* (Autumn 1960).

Pages 62-63: "A Damnation of Doves" from *The Birds of Pompeii*, copyright 1985 by John Ciardi, The University of Arkansas Press, Fayetteville; permission granted by Judith Ciardi.

Pages 64-65: "Winterpig." Denise Levertov: *Candles in Babylon*. Copyright © 1982 by Denise Levertov. Reprinted by permission of New Directions Publishing Corporation.

Page 68: "Drought" by Steven West. First published in *Number One*. Reprinted by permission.

Pages 68-69: "Killing the Rattlesnake" by Bill Brown. First published in *Number One*. Reprinted by permission.

Page 71: "Old Dog" from *Stories That Could Be True* by William Stafford. Copyright © 1977 by William Stafford. Reprinted by permission of Harper & Row, Publishers, Inc.

Pages 72-73: "Loyal" by William Matthews. From *A Happy Childhood* by William Matthews . Copyright © 1982, by William Matthews. By permission of Little Brown and Company.

Pages 73-74: "Mouse Elegy." From *The Gold Cell* by Sharon Olds. Copyright © 1987 by Sharon Olds. Reprinted by permission of Alfred A. Knopf, Inc.

Pages 75-76: "The Dead Calf" in *Openings*, copyright © 1968 by Wendell Berry, reprinted by permission of Harcourt Brace Jovanovich, Inc.

Pages 76-77: "The Southern Brown Recluse" by Walter McDonald. First published in *Creeping Bent*. Reprinted by permission of the author.

Page 78: "The Vixen" by Linda McCarriston. First published in *Talking Soft Dutch*, 1984. Lubbock, TX: Texas Tech University Press. Reprinted by permission.

Chapter 6

Pages 83-84: "Growing Up in the Nuclear Age" by Stephanie Johnston from *Junior Scholastic* (May 1984) and *Scholastic Voice* (May 1984). Reprinted by permission of Scholastic, Inc., and the author.

Pages 85-86: "Third World Primer" by Bill Brown. First published in *Number One*. Reprinted by permission.

Pages 87-88: "Instructions for a January Rainstorm" by Jennifer Drake from *Literary Cavalcade* (May 1986). Reprinted by permission of Scholastic, Inc., and the author.

Page 89: "Advice to My Niece" by Bill Brown. First published in *Riverstone*. Reprinted by permission.

Pages 89-90: "To David, About His Education" by Howard Nemerov from *The Next Room of the Dream*. Chicago, IL: University of Chicago Press.

Page 90: "To Cathy, Sleeping in My Second Hour Class Hamlet" by Richard Calisch in *English Journal,* November 1981. Copyright 1981 by the National Council of Teachers of English. Reprinted with permission of the publisher and the author.

Pages 91-92: "Lullabye for 17" is reprinted from *A Fraction of Darkness, Poems* by Linda Pastan, by permission of W.W. Norton & Company, Inc. Copyright © 1985 by Linda Pastan.

Pages 92-93: "About Women" by Judson Mitcham. First published in *The Georgia Review*. Reprinted by permission.

Chapter 7

Pages 95-96: "A Paper Bag" from *Two-Headed Poems* in *Selected Poems II: Poems Selected and New 1976–1986* by Margaret Atwood. Copyright © 1987 by Margaret Atwood. Reprinted by permission of Houghton Mifflin Company and Oxford University Press Canada.

Pages 100-102: "Poem in Which My Legs Are Accepted" from *What I Want?* by Kathleen Fraser, Harper & Row. Copyright © 1974 by Kathleen Fraser. Used by permission of Marian Reiner for the author.

Pages 102-103: "You Understand the Requirements" by Lyn Lifshin. Copyright © 1973 by Lyn Lifshin. From *Black Apples*. Trumansburg, NY: Crossing Press. Reprinted by permission of the author.

Pages 103-104: "Moving" from *Ungainly Things* by Robert Wallace. Copyright 1968 by Robert Wallace. Published by E. P. Dutton. Reprinted by permission of the author.

Pages 104-105: "How to Be Angry" by Sue Standing. First published in *Ploughshares*. Reprinted by permission of the author.

Pages 105-106: "Mirror" from *Crossing the Water* by Sylvia Plath. Copyright © 1963, 1971 by Ted Hughes. Reprinted by permission of Harper & Row, Publishers, Inc.

Pages 106-107: "The Man You Are Looking At" by Robert E. Haynes. Reprinted by permission of the author.

Chapter 8

Pages 109-110: "Landscape, 1986" by Paul McRay. First published in *passages north*. Reprinted by permission.

Page 110: "Two at the Library" by Gary Pacernik. First published in *Zone 3*. Reprinted by permission.

Pages 110-11: "In the All-Night Laundromat" by Ellen M. Taylor. First published in *passages north*. Reprinted by permission.

Page 117: "Aschenputtel" by Peter Stillman. © 1987 by Peter Stillman. From *Roth's American Poetry Annual 1988*. Reprinted by permission of the author and Roth Publishing, Inc.

Pages 118-19: "Subplot" by Jack Butler from *The Kid Who Wanted to Be a Spaceman*, August House Publishers, 1984. Originally appeared in *The New Yorker*, September 9, 1972. Reprinted by permission of the author.

Pages 119-20: "Revising History" by Gertrude Rubin. First published in *Jewish Currents*. Reprinted by permission.

Chapter 9

Pages 125-26: "Charit Creek" by Bill Brown. First published in *Number One*. Reprinted by permission.

Page 127: "Quiet Until the Thaw." Translated by Howard Norman from *Born Tying Knots: Swampy Cree Naming Stories* by Samuel Makidemewabe, 1976. Ann Arbor, MI: Bear Claw Press. Reprinted by permission of Howard Norman.

Page 128: "Got Dizzy." Translated by Howard Norman from *Born Tying Knots: Swampy Cree Naming Stories* by Samuel Makidemewabe, 1976. Ann Arbor. MI: Bear Claw Press. Reprinted by permission of Howard Norman.

Page 133: "Mary Nell" by Wendolyn Bozarth from *Scholastic Voice* (May 1986). Reprinted by permission of Scholastic, Inc., and the author.

Page 136: Lines from "The Housekeeper" by Robert Frost. Copyright 1930 by Holt, Rinehart and Winston and renewed 1958 by Robert Frost. Reprinted from *The Poetry of Robert Frost* edited by Edward Connery Lathem, by permission of Henry Holt and Company, Inc.

Pages 144-45: "Insomniac" by Sylvia Plath. Copyright © 1965 by Ted Hughes. From *The Collected Poems of Sylvia Plath*. Reprinted by permission of Harper & Row, Publishers, Inc.

Page 146: "Waking" from *Bone Love* by Malcolm Glass, 1979. Orlando: University of Florida Press. Reprinted by permission.

Pages 147-48: Lines from "Poem in October." Dylan Thomas: *Poems of Dylan Thomas*. Copyright 1945 by the Trustees for the Copyrights of Dylan Thomas. Reprinted by permission of New Directions Publishing Corporation.

Chapter 10

Page 152: "The Muse" by Tamarie Spielman. First published in *Number One*. Reprinted by permission.

Page 153: "Three Pencils at Frozen Head Creek" by Bill Brown. First published in *Number One*. Reprinted by permission.

Pages 155-56: "The Harbor" from *Chicago Poems* by Carl Sandburg, copyright 1916 by Holt, Rinehart and Winston, Inc. and renewed 1944 by Carl Sandburg, reprinted by permission of Harcourt Brace Jovanovich, Inc.

Pages 159-60: "County Lullabye" by George Scarbrough. First published in *Hogshead Review*. Reprinted by permission.

Pages 169-70: "Eighty" by Malcolm Glass. First published in *Sabal Palm Review*. Vol. 1, No. 1. Reprinted by permission.

Page 186: "Sonnet for the Blend of Music and Nature" by Tamarie Spielman. First published in *Amelia*. Reprinted by permission.

Introduction to the Writer

Anyone can write. That includes you. And this book will help you write as well as you can, perhaps even better than you think you can. The best way to become a better writer is by writing. Reading good writers is important, too; but along with reading, you have to do a lot of writing.

As you go through this book, you are going to find that your best writing is based on your own experience and told in your own voice.

For now you don't need to know much more; you can begin writing right away. Here's how to get started:

Begin every writing assignment by writing freely, quickly. Time yourself; don't let your pencil stop putting words on paper until you have written steadily for ten to fifteen minutes, or even more. This is called *fast-writing*. As you write, do not think about spelling, punctuation, or neatness. You can work on those things later. A fast-writing is like those quick drawings artists call "thumbnail" sketches. The natural flow of the pencil across the paper leads an artist to grace and control; and the flow of words onto the paper will give a writer grace and control, too.

If you get stuck while fast-writing and can't think what to say next, reread what you've just written; your own words will get you started again. If you find that you go off in a new direction, fine; go where your voice, your words, leads you.

It doesn't matter what form your writing takes on paper, either. You may write prose, or break your words into lines. What you write may not be a great piece of writing, or even a good piece—yet; so don't expect it to be. To give you an idea what a fast-writing is, take a look at this ten-minute example by Chris Bowman:

Last night we had chicken for the third time this week. Baked this time. Cluck, cluck. I think I'm growing feathers. Did your mother ever ask you to take that comb out of your hair? I hate this pencil. But I'm stuck with him. My true and only beloved pencil, wherefore art thou so dull? I hope no one sees this writing. I'd be so embarrassed. How can you say anything in ten minutes anyway? Did you know that the wind has two hemispheres? No. The brain, I mean. I am now writing from the left side of my head. My right side! Right? Yes. So all the hair on the right side of my head is kinking up in squiggly curls and the hair on the left side is going limp from lack of exercise. The photos Cam took of me are frightful. Is my nose really that crooked? The perils of playing basketball. Crunch. A flung elbow and a nose whacked out of shape. He says he likes it that way. Wish I did. Tonight we're going to that concert. Should I wear my mauve blouse? Silk. It's heavenly. He thinks so, too. What do I mean should I wear it? Of course, I should. Obviously. Just don't let me dribble chicken grease down the front.

—Chris Bowman

This piece came out as prose, and as a piece of writing it's rough, of course. It moves by fits and starts, the way the mind works as it sorts out things to say. At this point in the process that's probably to be expected.

The next example may seem more organized and unified because the writer tells a story, and narratives are relatively easy to organize; we're all born storytellers and we've done a lot of telling by the time we get out of the sixth grade. In this fast-writing Vicki Chezem recalls an experience of her childhood when she was asked to cure a case of "thresh" (actually *thrush*—a fungal infection of the mouth).

The old country folk call me "Thresh-healer" because my daddy died before I was born. I'm supposed to be able to perform minor miracles, like curing thresh in babies, removing warts, stopping bleeding, and several more I probably don't know about.

I must have been about five years old the first time they tried to make me heal someone. The neighbor's baby had thresh and the doctors didn't seem to be helping. I still remember that lady, 'Lisbeth, sitting in my Uncle-daddy's rocking chair with that baby laying across her altar-like lap. The baby was about level to my face, and my brothers grabbed my arms and dragged me over to that lady and tried to push my face down on the baby.

My mother and 'Lisbeth kept telling me to just blow in the baby's mouth so I could make it well. Surely I would help this poor little baby. I refused. I ran out of the room and hid in the kitchen, sure the sound of my heart beating would give me away. I hid beneath the wash stand.

I could hear my mother apologizing to 'Lisbeth and coming to get me, and my throat hurt and tears rolled down my cheeks. Please don't make me blow in that baby's mouth.

My mother came right to auntie's wash stand and pulled the curtain back and looked at me. She was so ashamed of me.

"Young lady, you are going to blow in that baby's mouth or I'm going to whip you."

I could see in her eyes that she meant it. I heard my Uncle-daddy walk into the kitchen. His voice was soothing, and he let me cling to him as he lifted me from beneath the wash stand, saying, "Let me talk to her, Joan."

So momma left the room and Uncle-daddy sat at the table with me on his lap and told me I didn't have to blow in that baby's mouth if I didn't want to. I lay against his chest, listening to his heart beat and loving that smell that was him, and meant security. After he had calmed me, he explained that the baby was sick and maybe I could help, and if I would, he'd take me down to the corner and get me a box of crackerjacks. Still, I didn't have to if I didn't want to, but it would make him happy if I did. Finally, he made everyone go away but 'Lisbeth and her baby, and he and I went into the living room and I blew into the baby's mouth.

—Vicki Chezem

The fact that Vicki's fast-writing is a story and seems more organized than Chris's doesn't necessarily make it better. The value of a fast-writing is not in polished lines but in rough ore. A fast-writing may be chaotic and crazy; but if it reveals a vein of experience that you can mine for good writing and rewriting, it will be valuable to you. And the only way to discover those veins is to keep writing. Sitting around thinking and worrying about it won't accomplish anything and may even bring on a bad case of writer's block.

We'll take that back. Thinking *does* help; of course it does. But it isn't directed and focused thinking that is most valuable as you begin a piece. Fast-writing in your head is a good idea; in fact, everybody spends a good portion of their lives doing it. Your mind is working constantly retelling to yourself things that have happened, should have happened, may happen. In a sense, daydreams are part of the process of composing, revising, and reexplaining that helps us make sense of what's going on in the world. When a poem falls onto the page already shaped, it is usually because you have been mulling over the material of the poem for days, months, maybe years.

Here is a fast-writing that came out as the draft of a poem. Perhaps it had been on the back burner of the writer's mind for a while:

Rituals

I rise every morning
and step onto the cold floor.
In the dark,
I reach down
and pull—
stretching muscle sinews
that move criss-crossed
as I try to touch the ceiling.
Outside
I hope the sun will rise again
to melt the frost
that holds the world,
closed,
like the sand
in the corners of my eyes
that keeps me
from waking
before my dreams dissipate,
humming a song
I wake hearing
and not knowing why.
I'll lay in bed
wanting to remember
the words
but the harder I try
the faster the music fades
until all I hear
is the purring of my cat—
asleep on the other pillow.
I'll pet her,
starting from the top
of her head
and pull my hand
down her neck.
I stop at the spot
where her back begins to arch.
I'll press its shedded hairs,
stuck to my palm,

against my closed eyes
hoping to absorb her sleep—
or at least enough
to allow me to drift off again
until the sun
reaches my window.

—Anonymous

Most of the time your fast-writings will come out as prose, sometimes in a voice you might use to talk to yourself—as Chris Bowman did—and sometimes in a voice you might use to talk to someone else. It doesn't matter how these initial pieces of writing sound, but when you decide to turn a fast-writing into a more finished piece, you will begin to think how a reader might react to your writing.

When you work with a fast-writing to make it a better piece (whether poetry or prose) you are writing a *draft*. After making changes, tightening, and rephrasing a few times, you will have a semifinal draft. (For some poets that may be draft no. 8 or no. 22!) Revision doesn't mean merely recopying; it means taking another look, reading through it looking for ways to rearrange phrases, to cut or sharpen words so your writing will be clearer, more pleasurable.

It's harder to revise a piece in your own handwriting. Typing puts a little distance between you and your words that makes it easier to see changes you need to make; so when you reach the semifinal stage, type it or print it neatly. Then put the draft away. When you come back to it a few days (or weeks) later, read it again and pencil in other changes and improvements. At this point you are fine-tuning, polishing.

Then (and only then) you should check the spelling and correctness. Proofreading is the very last step of the process and should be done only when you are ready for the final typing. Concentrating on the mechanical details earlier in the process of rewriting tends to clutter your mind and distract you from the more important changes and revisions you need to make. Have another person check for errors, too.

Now you should type a *final* draft, ready to be put up on the wall or sent to a friend, or an editor. Keep in mind, though, that for many writers the process of fine-tuning never ends. Even after a piece appears in print somewhere, you may see changes you will want to make to get a little closer to that perfection writers believe in, even though they know it isn't ever quite attainable.

Everything you write, every scrap, has some value. You never know when a part of a fast-writing or a phrase you've jotted down on the cover of your notebook may get you started on a good poem, story, or essay. Keep in a folder or notebook all of your fast-writings and drafts, notes, and doodles—ideas and phrases written on paper napkins, backs of envelopes, everything.

PS Before you launch into chapter 1, we invite you to read the following words of advice we have for your teacher. We encourage everyone to use this book in classrooms and workshops to develop a sense of community, colleagueship, and camaraderie; and your knowing something about the rationale behind the attitudes and practices of your teacher or group leader should help to achieve that goal.

Introduction to the Teacher

Please read the preceding "Introduction to the Writer," keeping in mind as you do that you, too, are a writer and that you should write the assignments in this book along with the students you are guiding. Here are some suggestions to make it easier for you to enable and help your students:

- It has been our experience that students write best as a community of writers. They can't always write together, but when they do, an audience outside their individual selves is established.

- Writing ideas should be discussed and models should be shared. Have the class read a section of a chapter to themselves. Then designate a group of two or three students to present each assignment. They might meet and decide what the writing idea involves so that they can discuss it with the class. Individuals should be familiar with each model poem and be prepared to read it out loud. (This will also encourage them to read their own pieces to each other.)

- The class should not spend too much time analyzing the poems. This is a writing class. Everyone should fast-write immediately after an assignment has been presented.

- Encourage them to honor each other's words and help them improve their writing by pointing out strengths and suggesting ways to improve a piece. (You might make it a rule that no one is allowed to say something derogatory about a fellow writer's work.)

You should make your work as evaluator easier by following these guidelines for reading and reacting to students' work:

- Have your students keep *all* their writing in folders, with each fast-writing, draft, and revision dated.

- Evaluate work by the honest effort and the effectiveness of a student's revisions. Letter grades on a draft will suggest that a poem is finished when it may not be. Give a letter grade for the growth and effort a student shows in a folderful of writing and/or a number of final drafts presented as a group of poems ready for readers outside the classroom.

- The assignments in this book are meant to be starters, guides to lead a writer toward a good piece of writing. No assignment should be an absolute requirement. Allow students to pass over one assignment in favor of another that interests them. Encourage them to try variations of assignments and to create assignments for themselves and their fellow writers. The variety of assignments and suggestions in this book should make it possible for writers to complete each chapter with a good many drafts added to their folders.

- Note mechanical errors only when a student is ready to type the final draft of a poem for presentation to an audience. Let the student do the work of correcting a piece and encourage students to help each other with proofreading. Writers learn the lessons of mechanics best when they make their own corrections *in the context of their own writing.*

- Tell your students when they begin this book that they should avoid meter and rhyme until they reach the last two chapters where such formal strictures are introduced. They must write a great deal of poetry in order to discover their own voices and to develop their powers of perception, imagination, and skills with language. Writing in strict meter and rhyme often inhibits this process and leads beginning writers to write clichés and empty sentiments for the sake of fulfilling a formal pattern.

The most important thing you can give writing students under your care is the power of belief:

- Do all you can to foster each student's belief that he or she *is* a writer. Your own expectations are important, too. You are likely to get good, imaginative writing if you expect it, if you keep saying, by implication and attitude, "Sure you can." Expect your students to be creative and perceptive and most of them will meet your expectations.

- Do all you can to give your students confidence. No one can become good at writing, or anything else, without it.

1

Haunting Your Childhood

Every time I go back to visit the small Tennessee town where I spent the first eighteen years of my life, I pass by the old Victorian house my family moved to when I was seven. A dentist lives there now. The apricot tree in the front yard is gone. The dogwoods my brother and I planted one spring are larger than I would have imagined. The house isn't white anymore but peach colored. I have longed to go inside and walk up the steps to the stairway window and look down into the hardwood forest tangled with honeysuckle.

There used to be a friendly ghost at that window which I created to protect me when I had to go upstairs to bed alone. Several years ago in a city hundreds of miles from my hometown, I awoke from a dream about that old house. I sat up in bed with pencil and paper to haunt the rooms of the house with my memory. The fast-writing turned into the first poem I ever published, and I learned that a building can be an important part of my emotional history.

A Change of Hands

At eight I would peep through the bedroom window
waiting for dripping hands to grab me in the dark,
scales and tail and wicked, knowing eyes.
Sometimes the hand of a ghost, cloud white,
would hold me with a soft terrible grasp.
But family noises from below
reminded me soon those gentle calloused
hands would tuck me in goodnight.

1

Morning brought a window draped in oak-filtered
light which scanned my handiwork
of weeded snapdragons and rose
and looked out to honeysuckle
caves where I staged my fondest
childhood fights.

At thirty-four I crept up the stairs past the room
where one March night my Father's calloused hands
clutched his heart and fell limp,
past the attic stairway to my room
where in a familiar window
I found the backyard swept
of honeysuckle caves
where children no longer hide
and the only hands I could
conjure up to hold me
were my own.

—B. B.

Think back into the past as far as you can and remember the first
house you lived in. If you were very young and your memories are
faint, then recall the next house or apartment. If you have always
lived in the same place, go back to your earliest vivid memories. Now
draw the floor plan of the house or apartment. Don't worry about
how artistic your drawing is, but do put in everything you can remember—rooms, closets, the doorways, stairways, windows. Include the
location of some of the furniture, if you can. You might draw separate
sketches of the basement, the attic, the upstairs, if your house had
them. If you're remembering an apartment, you might sketch the
hallways, the parking lot, laundry room, anyplace nearby that was
part of your home.

Look at your plan, then close your eyes and travel back. Walk
through the house like an invisible spirit. Now take the same journey
on paper. Quickly write your way through the house, describing the
rooms, the furniture, the people you find, and the things they once
did there—the place the dog stained the rug, the wall you scrawled on
with your sister's crayon, the grease fire your mother put out with a
raincoat.

Read through your fast-writing and put an asterisk in the margin
beside the most memorable places and events. Which of them made
you most happy, frightened, embarrassed, ashamed, angry? Pick one
of them and relive it, writing your way freely through the experience.
Let it happen again—on paper.

If your fast-writing stalls or runs out of gas, reread it and see if you can get a fresh start where you stopped. If that doesn't work, find another asterisk and write that memory.

SECRET PLACES

I am always amazed at the insignificant but magical places of the house I grew up in. I could step into my closet, close the door, pull the light chain, and fly my closet anywhere I imagined. In the following poems students found closets that were important to their childhood. While writing the poems, each found a secret or insight still lurking there.

Epiphany

The closet in your room was a white walk-in
with a shoe rack up the wall
where me and my brother played pirates
swinging from the crow's nest.
I used to run in and jump on the bed to wake you
(get up Lazybones)
and giggle while you rolled out from under a pillow
warming your nostrils with the coffee smell
that trickled in from the kitchen.
Later, I would shiver into my clothes
by the electric heater in the dining room
while you left for work.
Mom would take us to school, my brother and me,
and I would forget all about you
until you came back home for dinner.
I remember complaining because I wanted
to sit by Mom, not you,
but it took me all these years
to see the hurt in your eyes.

—Stephanie Johnston

My Name Is Makela

When I was 5
I decided my name was Debbie
and wouldn't answer
to any other name.

I remember one Saturday morning
when Mom was making bread
asking her how to spell it.
I asked her a couple of times
so I got it right.
Tam (my sister)
wasn't in her room
so I went into her closet
into the back corner
where I thought nobody'd ever find it
and wrote Debbie 3 times
with different crayons.
On Sunday morning
Mom, Dad, and Tam
came to me to ask
if I'd written in Tam's closet.
I said no and accused Tam
of doing it and blaming me.
They finally gave up
and said it would stay written there
until I admitted it.
I went to my room
and listened to Tam
yelling that it wasn't fair
that I should get off that easily
and smiled.
But soon guilt crept over me
like an afternoon shadow
and I worried
that my parents wouldn't love me
anymore.
I drew a picture of a girl
with long curly brown hair
and tears bigger than her eyes
rolling down her face
to her unhappy red mouth
and labeled it "MAKELA."
Then I took it to Tam
and she wrote what I dictated–
"I am sorry I did not tell you
I wrote on the wall."
I took it downstairs
to my parent's bedroom

and gave it to my dad.
Mom was taking a shower.
I can still remember Dad
opening the bathroom door
to show the picture to Mom
and how the steamy air
crept over me
and out the open window
taking my guilt with it.

—Makela Spielman

Look at your house plan. Identify the places where you played—corners, closets, porch swings, attics, basements—places that held mystery, places you weren't supposed to play in. Find the child's voice like Makela; or, if you wish, tell it from the distance of age, seeing now from older eyes, as Stephanie did.

MEMENTOS

Childhood is the perfect place for a poet to look for things to write about. As children we met each new experience with an eager sense of wonder and discovery. These are qualities a writer must keep alive. As long as you live, each moment has the potential for excitement, fear, or joy. Society seems to say, "Grow up; don't be silly and childish." But we all need to stay in touch with the child we used to be so that life will continue to surprise and delight us. Otherwise, everything gets boring. A writer's main task is allowing discovery to happen—to him- or herself, to anyone who reads what he or she has written. A writer's gift to others is reminding them that they have not lost the capacity to be amazed at the world around them. Writing about childhood makes this job remarkably easy.

In the following poem a high school student found an old rosary in a box hidden in her closet. It no longer serves any religious or practical purpose, but she has kept it for years. In this object she found a fragment of memory and a child's voice to tell a story that needed to be told.

The Gift

I have a best friend named Rosita
who wasn't born in America.
Her family drove here
and now they just live next door.

While the grass was still wet we would sneak
back behind the honeysuckle
and there was our castle
with just enough room to stand
and do a wild dance.
She had a brown rattle.
Sometimes in my basement
she would be the King of France
and I would be the King of Egypt
and we would duel.

I gave Rosita a piece of my skin
and she gave me a piece of hers.
We twisted them around ourselves,
so that we were striped.
And no one could tell us there was a difference,
not even my sister.
Rosita and me, we knew.
But no one else would understand,
if they looked,
why I have a rosary in my closet,
or why she has
a white-faced rag doll.

—Eleanor Womack

Do you have objects that you have held on to for a while? A rock,
a watch, a letter, an old pair of cowboy boots, a doll? Close your eyes
and find their hiding place. Objects radiate with the emotional power
we invest in them. When you open your eyes, begin to write as quickly
as you can, keeping the image of the object in your head. You can
describe it, tell where you found it, why you keep it. Start anywhere,
and then follow your writing wherever it leads you.

SEASONS OF THE HOUSEHOLD

Read "The Coming of Winter." Notice how the wool coat holds past
stories and places that wind through the poem, tying it together. As
you flow with the words in Amy's poem, see, smell, and feel the
images of winter.

The Coming of Winter

Once a year
we head to the closets

to search the back corners
where mice have chewed holes
in the old wooden walls.
We reach for last year's plastic bags
that bulge to overflowing
with woolen mittens
and snowball-topped caps
that Grandma knitted.
Everything holds a musty smell,
the Navy pea jackets
dusty with the age
of summertime spent hidden away—
a ghost who died last year.
Somehow they remind me of the snow
blown like delicate feathers
clinging to the navy blue
until, like magic, they disappear
into tiny beads of water
between a few stray threads of wool.
I caught them
as I ran down the beach
at Lake Michigan
where wind blew past my clothes
to my numb-cold skin
and I had to climb back up the trail
to our little green cottage.
        (I waited for another day
        when the sun shone brighter.)
And there were winters
when we'd all pile onto one sled
and race down the hill
behind our house
past the pear tree
and the dry blackberry briars
to the creek
where Mom
cracked through the ice
and skinned her face—
        It bled down the collar
        of her wool coat—
Now I pull the narrow arms
close around mine
feeling the satin lining
cling to my sweat-dampened skin

and the Navy-rough wool
scratch against my neck
like the coming of winter.

—Amy Evans

Did you smell the "mustiness" of the wool jacket, hear "the crack
of ice," and see snowflakes "disappear / into tiny beads of water /
between a few stray threads of wool"? These concrete images make
the poem authentic. See, hear, feel, and smell the sensory impressions you remember, and write down their details. It doesn't matter
whether what is being reported is memory, invention, or a combination of both. The details will help make your writing convincing, for
they help draw the reader closer to perceiving the experience.

Some of the best poems have been inspired by the seasons. Start
with a particular place like an attic, a closet, or porch. Let an old
sweater, a pair of boots, or sled take you away. Pay attention to small
details, like the smell of burning leaves in fall or the glare of icicles in
the morning sun. Let weather and images be a jumping-off place; then
let the sensory details carry you wherever they will.

WEATHER WORDS

Here's a poem written from a window in the present rather than the
past. Notice how the writer lets the window be the wind's eye to carry
her into the sounds, smells, sights, and feelings of the season, the
weather, and the place.

November Rain

From my window
I can hear the creek rising
as it pushes against mud banks
and the raindrops form rings
tightly woven on the smooth-running surface.
One time the water reached high enough
to flood the old dirt-floored barn
that used to house the mules and chickens.

I remember it rushed so strong
carrying away the bridge my dad built,
the one his maple-branch walking stick
hit against hard with rage

sounding like a gunshot
through the autumn hills
the day the gang of neighbors' dogs
tore the dirty white feathers from our blind rooster
and he lay there
shivering in the water
that carried his blood away.
I have watched the creek flood
and watched it carry trees downstream.

I have heard the beat of rain
falling outside my window
and closed my eyes tightly
to hear the storm closing in.

—Amy Evans

Is there a window, porch rocker, or back stoop where you have watched a bad storm coming or listened to a soft autumn rain tap on fallen leaves? Everyone has watched a yard fill up with snow or the glassy reflection lights make on wet night streets. Close your eyes and imagine a time when you felt the loneliness of weather and write.

TELLING IT BACK, I

Before you talk about a poem (whether already published or freshly drafted), you should be sure you understand the content; and telling another reader what you think the poem is about is the best way to see if you do.

You should always begin discussing any poem with a five-minute session of "telling it back." Get together a group of four or five people and have someone read this poem by Gary Snyder:

Marin-An

sun breaks over the eucalyptus
grove below the wet pasture,
water's about hot,
I sit in the open window
& roll a smoke.

distant dogs bark, a pair of
cawing crows; the twang
of a pygmy nuthatch high in a pine—

from behind the cypress windrow
the mare moves up, grazing.

a soft continuous roar
comes out of the far valley
of the six-lane highway—thousands
and thousands of cars
driving men to work.

—Gary Snyder

Your group should practice telling it back, using these steps:

1. Begin by having someone in the group say who the speaker, or
   persona, of the poem is. You can't be very specific about the
   speaker of "Marin-An" because you can't tell things like the
   speaker's age or occupation. Perhaps you will start by saying,
   "The speaker of the poem is a person who . . . " Now what *can*
   you say about the speaker? Get it said in a phrase or two.

2. The next step is to tell back the content of the poem. This is
   sometimes called paraphrasing, restating in your own words
   what the speaker says. If there is a story line, simply retell what
   happens, in a brief plot summary. In "Marin-An" there isn't much
   of a plot because the poem is mostly description, but you can tell
   what the speaker describes, going through the poem from beginning to middle to end. Is there an implied contrast between the
   first two stanzas and the last one? If so, that should be included
   in your telling of the poem.

   Have a couple of people in the group try to tell back the poem;
   the rest of you can decide who does it best.

2

The Old Neighborhood

In the Australian Oak
—*for my mother*

Mid-Atlantic, I climbed
out of my cockpit and shinnied
up the struts to the upper
wing, where I stood on flimsy
fabric, braced by the
thinnest limbs, the topmost
leaves brushing my face.

The wind leaned me out,
over palm trees thirty feet
below, their fronds arcing
in fountains to the grass
swimming away to the house,
to the kitchen window
where my mother stood
peeling carrots.
I did not believe falling
was possible, yet she
knew . . . and still let me
ride the dare. She held me
safe across the ocean
and the ice wind.

—M. G.

Saturdays I woke early, scrambled into jeans and sneakers, then stared out my bedroom window to see if any of my friends had beat me outside. I closed my eyes and in my imagination made the rounds to all the important places in my neighborhood: the hideout in the honeysuckle hedge, the tree house in Linda Jo's backyard, the drainage ditch we called a creek, and the scrap-wood fort behind the Brighams' barn. There were forbidden places too, like the funeral home garage where my brother Clark locked Becky Robinson in an old casket. Some mornings I escaped the house before my mother could force me to drink my milk and eat my oatmeal. Each day was a clean slate, where, like in a good poem, anything could happen.

Brainstorm and jot down a list of old neighborhood places important to your childhood—trees, garages, playgrounds, parks, creeks, forbidden danger zones, hideouts, haunted places, places where exciting, magical things happened. Then write down events—accidents, frequent games, the deepest snow, the great flood, the terrible fire, the new neighbor, anything out of the ordinary. Now, choose one and write as quickly as you can. Let the people, sights, sounds, and feelings of the old neighborhood take you with them.

Fright

The accident.
The branch broke
and I fell,
hitting my legs
on the concrete blocks.

I yelled and when she didn't come,
staggered, bloody-kneed,
to the house.
I pounded on the door,
the dog bouncing around
my knobby knees and scarlet shins.
She hadn't heard me!
She hadn't heard me!

I still carry the white scars
of her disbelief.

—Wendolyn Bozarth

Often the most trivial accidents stay in our memory. Even our bodies carry their scars. Find an accident that happened to you or to someone you knew. Capture the immediacy of the event, the action, the concrete details and the feelings surrounding it. Tell the event on paper and see if writing about it helps you understand why you remember it.

Some accidents are small like the one in "Fright." In "Pulled Out of Bed," a student remembers a more dramatic event.

Pulled Out of Bed

Pulled out of bed,
long after day had ended,
my eyes screamed against the yellow light
and frigid air.
But I had to come and watch the show,
you said.
I knew the look in your eyes.
Wearing quilts around our shoulders
we pounded up the driveway
to the smooth street,
our naked feet slapping the pavement
still warm from yesterday's sun.
I held onto the mailbox for support
as the world over the hill
shot into flames
and outlined the empty black arms of trees
like fragile skeletons of fish
against the molten sky.
Holding your arms tightly,
I felt the smoky air under my eyelids.
Water rolled down my face to touch my lips.
We heard muted voices.
The neighbors stood
with silent hands
as the fire ate the barn slowly,
savoring each ember,
it was beautiful,
before the sirens came.

—Tracey Tomlinson

Can you recall any big happenings like the disaster described in the previous poem? Think of the setting, the time of day or night. What people were involved? As you write, use as many concrete details as possible, like "the pavement / still warm from yesterday's sun." Use comparisons to help capture the moment, such as "the world over the hill / shot into flames / and outlined the empty black arms of trees / like fragile skeletons of fish." Simple and subtle images, such as "the neighbors stood with silent hands," can be effective, too. As you write let your voice relive this experience.

SPECIAL PLACES

When Theodore Roethke was a child, his family ran a plant nursery. As you read the next poem, pay close attention to the wonderful use of sounds and images. His description fills a quiet, dark root cellar with action and pungent smells.

Root Cellar

Nothing would sleep in that cellar, dank as a ditch,
Bulbs broke out of boxes hunting for chinks in the dark,
Shoots dangled and drooped,
Lolling obscenely from mildewed crates,
Hung down long yellow evil necks, like tropical snakes.
And what a congress of stinks!—
Roots ripe as old bait,
Pulpy stems, rank, silo-rich,
Leaf-mold, manure, lime, piled against slippery planks.
Nothing would give up life:
Even the dirt kept breathing a small breath.

—Theodore Roethke

While some poems center around events, "Root Cellar" focuses on the place itself. Can you remember a place where you went when you needed to be alone, away from accidents, chores, or neighborhood games? Recall the spot you enjoyed most because it was yours. Start writing by being specific: tell whether it was hidden away in an alley, on a roof, or in the middle of a field under a tree. Then let the smells, sights, sounds, and feelings of the place help you bring it to life again.

SPECIAL TREASURES

Lost Treasure

The Abingdons died here in '32,
scattered all around the yard like oranges

shot out of the trees. They left black
stains in the sand and—somewhere—
a hundred thousand in cash from their last
bank heist. The house still stands, a dark
music only the pines understand, all
its interior walls and flooring torn

down and out when the McGregors
owned the place. They didn't find the money,
so maybe it is buried near one
or another of those live oaks out back.
Remember those maps in the adventure
books? Pirates followed the dotted lines
fifty paces north from the crooked palm,
then east to the patch of sand marked

with an X like a black iron cross.
But the Abingdons left no map. And now
only the trees remember how many steps
tell the spot. Late at night we wander
among the trees, weaving a pattern
which means nothing, leads nowhere.
Under a windless shard of moon, we hear
one tree whining, twisting and creaking

as though laden with ice in a hard
winter storm—some pirate lost in a maze
of steps and charmed into the trunk,
or one of the Abingdons, his unrepentant soul
caught in the branches, crying over lost coins.
Following the only lead we have, we dig
midnight to dawn and beyond, broken
by breaking roots, and end nagged

to distraction by aching muscles, and not
one penny richer. Wind has gained strength
and above us, the tree has changed its tune.
Whoever brought us to this spot is cruel
as well as unremorseful. No less greedy
than the robbers, we have nothing
to do but join in with our own laughter.

—M. G.

When I was eight, I saw the movie *Treasure Island*. For a year I
combed the ground for pirate *X*'s that marked the spot of buried

treasure. Behind my grandmother's house was an old hill where it was rumored that a confederate soldier had buried a chest of silver dollars. One summer my sister and I dug an entire day until my father made us come in for supper. I guess no one ever found that silver, but as I dug, every rock I hit was a potential fortune. I felt the excitement of the unexpected, like searching an attic or creeping through the rooms of an abandoned house. We'd have dug all week if he hadn't made us resod the hill the next morning.

Did you ever search for treasure? If so, relive the account with words and see what happens. If not, remember the kid you were and have at it this time. There's no telling what you might discover.

SPECIAL CHARACTERS

Clayton Bloom Came Mornings

Clayton Bloom came mornings up
our only street, red Bruno pulling him.
The dog, like Clayton's coat, was oversize,
a bear, its ruff-cowled
anvil skull concluding in a leer.

Clayton's ancient habit was to pause
a dozen times to argue with the wind,
or chat with people no one else could see.
Bruno's was to churn at flank-speed to
the store, his master jerking like
an empty skiff behind. And so
their daily going seemed a metaphor,
with Clayton's rearing back no more
than what a man must do against his fate.

The red dog always wins, of course.
Some trifling malady dragged Clayton in
his flapping coat to death, who didn't know
his age or how to read a clock, and told
me once that doctors had "sawed off" his heart
when he was still a boy. Perhaps, therefore,
he went less vexed and terrified
than others buried on the hill.

—Peter Stillman

Where I grew up in West Tennessee, Clayton Bloom would have been called "a character," or just "curious." Two houses down from where I lived as a boy, an elderly man named old Mo sat on the porch swing all day and whittled. He got along better with dogs and cats than he did with people. Early in the morning we could hear him whistle. I've never heard anyone whistle that beautifully since.

Most neighborhoods have their characters. They don't have to "argue with the wind," or die without knowing their age to be considered different. Who was the character in your neighborhood? What strange behaviors did you observe that makes you think so? Did other people tell stories about this person? We're not trying to spread gossip or rumors. There's nothing wrong with being different. But characters' lives make good stories and poems. Begin by placing the person in a setting which is natural, like "Clayton Bloom came mornings up / our only street." Then, remembering what you have seen and heard, build your character by describing the person's appearance and actions. Make your writing rich with particular detail and behavior.

TELLING IT BACK, II

Take the best draft you have written so far and get together with two other students. (They should have their best drafts, too.) Read your poem aloud or have someone read it for you. Then ask the other two to "tell it back," using these steps:

1. One listener should tell who the speaker is. Be brief and fairly general: the speaker of "My Name Is Makela" (in chapter 1) is simply a girl remembering an incident in her childhood.

2. The other listener should tell, briefly, what the poem is about, going from the beginning to the middle, and then to the end. If he or she were telling back "My Name Is Makela," it might go something like this: "The girl tells about trying to blame her sister for her own wrongdoing and then feels guilty and confesses the truth. At the end of the poem she apologizes and that helps her feel less guilty." However the listener says it, he or she should be brief and to the point.

    Rule: You, the poet of this draft, can't say anything until the others are through; it's not fair to coach or help them out, by saying things like, "No, what I meant was . . . "

3. After your readers have finished telling back your poem, each of them should point out the parts he or she liked best.

The point of this sharing back and forth is for you to find out which passages of the poem worked well and which parts weren't clear. When your readers hit a part of your poem they can't tell back, you have a problem. You should work on that part, putting in more detail, perhaps, or removing excess detail. That way readers won't lose the thread of the story or miss the scene you want them to see. You might start revising your draft by writing down what it was you were going to say when you found yourself wanting to break in with "But I meant . . . "

Get together with other writers often for sessions like this; everyone benefits—not only as writers, but as readers. And don't pick the same folks every time; you'll gain more from a variety of reactions to your work.

PULLED OUT—AGAIN

Go back to the beginning of this chapter and reread Tracey Tomlinson's poem, "Pulled Out of Bed." Now read the selection below, part of a section in Peter Stillman's book of poetry and prose, *Gilead: Notes on a Catskill Hamlet:*

George's Place

Late in the night of December 27th the fire siren went off. It is a terrible sound to wake to—raw, ugly, insistent. I don't, this time, have to wonder what or where the blaze is. As I hurry into clothing and boots in the dark of the livingroom, I see the awful brightness of open flame in the windows of a small, shabby house diagonally across the road. In the approximately two minutes it takes me to dress and dash out the door, the front of the place erupts in a sheet of fire, and blazing pieces of siding and shingles loft in the wind, come floating down on nearby rooftops. The firehouse is just across the way, and as I run up, engines are coughing to life, men are throwing on turn-out gear, snatching up equipment, stringing hoses from pumper to house. Despite the proximity, it is already too late; the fire has gotten to the house's vitals. It's about five above zero; even the men who are properly dressed suffer miserably, for we fight the thing until nearly 4:30, joined by others from three nearby districts. When we're done, we've emptied six tankers and a large pond. One of our trucks has blown its pump, four hoses have frozen and ruptured, a score of firefighters have been injured or sickened by smoke. The Rescue Squadron ambulance from Summit has been standing by most of the night, dispensing oxygen and first aid. My coat is sheathed in ice; whenever I've been relieved, I've stood shaking uncontrollably. Others are in similar condition. The Women's Auxiliary passes out coffee and doughnuts, and Butch has thought to run whiskey down from his tavern.

It has been a grim night's work but somehow stirring too. I don't like fires and wouldn't walk around the corner to see one. Always after a big, nasty blaze, though, I get a funny lump in my throat. There's no way to put it without sounding softheaded. You'd have to be there in the dark, I suppose, hanging on to a bucking three-inch high-pressure hose, slipping on the ice forming underfoot, moving closer and closer into the stinking, searing ugliness of a fire, gagging on the smoke, taking back into your face, down your collar and sleeves most of the stale, frigid water that bounces from walls and roof, to know how powerfully you begin to love the black-coated fellow next to you. I can't explain the intimacy—why, even after the fire is out, men linger, despite the hour, the drenched and reeking clothes, the exhaustion—why they are reluctant to go home. It never fails to touch me. Nothing else about a fire is any good at all.

—Peter Stillman

Stillman's piece is a journal entry he has turned into a prose excursion or personal essay. In his book Stillman uses both poetry and prose to give his reader notes and observations on the community where he lives. In this case he decided to use prose to relate the experience of the fire and his feelings and thoughts about it. Tracey Tomlinson wrote her account of the fire in her neighborhood as a poem. What's the difference?

Before you read any further, sit down with a couple of other people who have read these pieces and work together to make a list of differences you can see. Put down anything, even if it seems obvious (like the fact that the poem is written in lines of varying length, while the prose is right-justified). There are other differences. Some may seem trivial; others, more important. Put down everything your group can think of.

Now have your group make a list of the similarities—the obvious (they are both about a fire in the speaker's neighborhood) and the not so obvious (both of these selections use particular images to help the reader see and experience an event).

After you have made your lists, continue reading here.

You may have noticed that Peter comments on the meaning of the event he relates, whereas Tracey doesn't. This distinction is worth thinking about because it is often a major difference between prose and poetry. Peter talks *about* the "intimacy" of sharing the experience of watching and fighting a fire; Tracey *implies it* through the image "Holding your arms tightly" and the line "I knew the look in your eyes." Tracey suggests emotion by describing the neighbors standing "with silent hands"; Peter presents emotion a little more directly by *telling* us the experience gave him a funny lump in his throat.

These differences don't mean that one piece of writing is better than the other; they show, simply, that they are *different*. It may be that a writer who decides to write in prose is more intent, sometimes, on things he has to say—ideas, information—and wants to make sure he gets those ideas across to the reader briefly and directly. The writer who chooses to write a poem may be more intent on giving her reader the emotions an experience evoked; she wants to make sure she gets those emotions across to the reader briefly and *in*directly.

Keep in mind, as you write your way through this book, that you may write either prose or poetry. Many times your first fast-writing may be prose. When you turn the fast-writing into a draft, you may find it becomes a prose excursion or essay, rather than a poem. Follow your impulse; listen to your intuition; let your piece of writing help you find its own shape and form.

You might even try, every once in a while, to write the same writing assignment in *both* poetry and prose. If you do that, notice differences in the two versions, and the similarities, too. You can learn a great deal about writing (and reading) simply by paying attention to your own writing and *your* ways of working at it.

3

Photograph
Album

On a shelf in front of me is a faded brown photograph, probably taken around the turn of the century, which I bought for a dollar at an antique mall (known to many people as a junk shop). In this portrait are three people I know nothing about—a bearded man sitting with a young boy on his lap and an older boy standing beside him.

The best poems often come most easily from the things we know and care about. But what if I let my imagination play with the possibilities waiting to be discovered in this photograph? Let me see where my pencil takes me.

Red silk, faded now, brown, rusted iron, black trousers turned to the brown of faded photographic paper. Maroon and gray overcast with tan. Yellow, the color of the pages of old books. Freckled. Sunspots. The photo. He looks like an editor I once knew, like a purchasing agent I know now. The man is wearing boots—motorcycle boots. The boys wear high-top shoes. They'd be in fashion today. The lace collars and satin coats would look strange, though. The older boy looks like my sister-in-law at that age. The small boy is leaning back as though he's about to go to sleep, his mouth open as though he might burp. What is it about this picture that is so blah and uninteresting? Perhaps the older son grew up to be a murderer or a banker. The young boy was a missionary to Africa. The father owned a general store. He died of a fever in the midst of dreams of flour sacks pressing against his chest. The boys did not weep at his bedside. He had, after all, been a cruel man. The boys wept at his bedside. He had, after all, been a kind and generous man. The man stares out of this photo at the camera almost mournfully. He was a widower. The mother of the boys died in childbirth. And the infant girl died with her. The man seems unconcerned with the boys, as though they aren't there with him at all. He is remembering the girl he married, her eyes like cornflowers; he even told her that one time. He is thinking of the girl with blue eyes who never grew to womanhood, never found a boy to fall in love with her eyes, never had a child, never died in childbirth.

Well, you see how it goes with fast-writings. I got off to a slow start, the way pieces of writing often do at first; then I wandered a bit as I followed a train of thought, backed up to go another way. As I approached the end, I think my imagination was beginning to breathe some life into these two-dimensional figures. It's interesting that the liveliest actions and characters in my writing are not in the picture at all. There may be a poem to be found in this photo—or possibly a short story, or an essay. I should come back in a few days and write again, perhaps using the end of this writing as a jumping-off place.

Photographs about people and events more familiar and more important to a writer can be even better places to start on the search for a poem.

SNAPSHOTS

Go photo hunting. Search old albums, yearbooks, and drawers for elementary school class pictures, shots of the family at reunions or holidays, or pictures of people you don't remember or even know. Keep them safe in an envelope or folder and carry them with you. You might talk about the photos with parents, grandparents, sisters, and brothers to jog your memory. Find out what you can about the people, the places, the occasion. If it is a school picture, talk to the other people in it, if you can. If you don't have an actual photo, use your internal camera. Close your eyes and visualize people as they were, as they might have been. Recall the expressions on their faces, the clothes they wore.

In the following poem, the persona speaks to the members of her class: "Marilyn afraid / of blowing off the page"; "George the star . . ."; and a student who is gone, "Eileen, . . . unable to fit / the corners to those of earth."

Yearbook

They look through the light the color
of burnt grass,
for tufts of morning.
The shower of comments
from teachers and classmates
isn't enough to wash away
the rust. Marilyn afraid
of blowing off the page holds
the flagpole. George the star:
chin clamped like the top
of a desk, thoughts stuck
in hoops far off.
Eileen has moved out of her
frame, unable to fit
the corners to those of earth.
Along the edge of distance
she bends over rainbarrels.

I've nothing to give you still
parched on your page except
the aisles between words.

—Sister Mary Lucina

Now read Jill Baumgaertner's poem.

Upon Finding a Photo of
My Second Grade Class

She sits in the front row middle of the second grade,
ankles crossed.
Her dress perfectly pressed.
Her shoes brown oxfords.
Her smile reticent but never wavering.
This is the child of the long walks home
swinging her
satchel, watching the corner for its
turn and the great
green house and mother waiting
sipping cokes on the
front porch.
The pecans cracked in the back yard,
the piles of father's scratch paper in the closet,

the smell of a house just painted,
her hair drying
in front of a gas heater,
singed hair her mother combs
out and in the apartment over the garage a man and
woman
with their blonde coffee table
and plate-size ashtrays.
This is the one I am and am now mother to.
This little one
without real eyes
just a play of greys and whites,
her dress a pattern
her classmates shadows
already crumbling into the brick
background of
Salias Mahone Elementary School.

—Jill P. Baumgaertner

Notice how the narrator speaks of her second-grade self in third person: "She sits in the front row . . . ," "Her dress perfectly pressed . . . ," "This is the child of the long walks home. . . ." See how she recalls the rich sensory details of the pecans cracked in the back yard, the piles of father's scratch paper, the smell of a house just painted.

What does she mean by the line "This is the one I am and am now mother to"?

In the last part of the poem, the narrator shifts from third person to first. She identifies herself as the little girl and also as the mother to the little one now. How does this shift affect what the poem says to you?

Here are some ideas to help you write more drafts from pictures:

1. Look at your old school pictures or close your eyes and visualize the class, especially the faces. Can you recall any specific events? Begin your fast-writing by talking to your former classmates about the things you recall most vividly.

2. Look at your own picture. Address the child you were in the third person. Go through an event the picture evokes in your memory or the routines of an ordinary day. You might make a brief list of sensory images you can recall: the smell of burning leaves, the sound of the dog barking at the mailman, or your father singing in the shower. Somewhere in the poem, if it feels right, shift to

first person and speak to the child you were. If that doesn't work, let your fast-writing take you wherever it will.

THE EVENT IN THE MOMENT

In the following poem the narrator looks at an old photograph and remembers the time that he and his dad gigged a gar. Read this poem carefully and imagine you are the speaker looking at the photo that you hadn't thought about in years.

Gar

On the lawn of Bishopstead
we stand, fading, our paper skin
turning sepia. We give the camera
twisted faces, squinting against
the glare spread over Florida,
our feet rooted in the ragged
grass. What seems at first
a railing we lean on
is the shaft of the gig,
and at Dad's end, the gar,
a slab of leather and cussedness
struck through his middle
with the barbed tines.

Before, we had hunted them
at night, drifting down
the canals between the lakes
under the starless ceiling
of palms and oak trees,
gig poised for a gar snaking
into the corridor of light.

And then this one, caught
on film, as though we knew
it would be our only trophy,
hit right off the dock at noon,
nailed in the eye of the sun.

—M. G.

Choose one of your photos that implies an action or an event. What happened that day and what does it mean to you now? Does it

feel strange to remember, almost as if it were in another lifetime? In
your fast-writing include the details of this event. You might start with
the immediacy of the moment, the way this poem opens: "On the
lawn of Bishopstead / we stand . . . "

SECONDHAND WRITING

I'm a sucker for thrift shops. I've found some of my most prized shirts
and coats this way. One day I bought an old wool jacket and, in one
of the pockets, found a photograph of a family celebration. I felt as if
I had accidentally stumbled into a private party, uninvited. I wondered about the people and the occasion. Was it a wedding, Fourth of
July picnic, or a birthday? I wrote a poem about these people being
locked in time. Later my class gave me a group of old photos bought
at a flea market. We put them up on a board and wrote about the
people. We asked what their life was like, and tried to find something
in their dress, posture, or facial expressions that might reveal personalities and relationships. Some wonderful writing came from this
experience.

Choose a few photographs of people from your folder that no one
in your class will recognize—the older the better. As a class, mix them
up and display them on a board. Discover what important conversations and stories your imagination can shape through your fast-writings. Leave them up a week or more so you can return to them from
time to time.

SUGGESTED FOLLOW-UP ASSIGNMENT

In the following poem, a student was shown an old picture of his
great-great-grandfather. While describing his features and dress, the
narrator recalls a story about his relative during the Civil War.

Neutral Territory

I sat at the table in my grandmother's dining room.
The noise of the dinner had died down
in quiet anticipation of the dessert to come.
My father was looking at an old picture
which my grandfather had handed him.
When he was finished,
he handed it to me

and I held it gently in my hands
to avoid hurting the cracked edges.

The picture was of my
great-great-grandfather.
He had a long beard
which seemed to be attached
to the breast of his coat.
His hair was curly
and brushed back from his face
and was the style of the time.
His expression was stern
but his eyes seemed kind and caring.
All this was caught
over a century ago
by the click of a shutter.

He had been a carpenter by trade
and several houses which he had built
still stand in the area
near Whitestone, Tennessee.
I had visited one of those houses,
two story with a porch that stuck out into the yard.
My great-great-grandfather had lived there
during the war
and it is said that he would cross
into Yankee territory
to visit his family.
He would hide his horse
and spend the night with his wife and children.
Because there were Yankee patrols in the area
he would keep his gun near.

Early in the morning
before the sun had risen,
he would say farewell
and leave under cover of darkness.
He knew that he would be safe
once he crossed the river
into neutral territory.
His family,
expecting the loud crack of a shot
to pierce the silence,
would wait in fear

until they could hear
the sound of his horse
clattering across the bridge.

—Josh Culley

Find a picture of a relative you never met, perhaps one who lived before you were born. Let the details of the photograph draw you into the life and times of the person. Have you heard stories about this relative? Find out what your ancestors did for a living, where they came from, what troubles or successes they experienced. Blend in anything you have heard about them with your description of the person. If you can't find any old photos, your writing can be based on what you have heard about your relatives, or on stories you make up.

END-STOPPING

As you write these assignments, you may be getting your words down as prose—letting the right edge of the page tell you when to start a new line.

Or . . . you may be breaking your fast-writing into lines of varying length, ending the lines wherever it seems right so that it looks like a free-verse poem from the very start.

No matter which way you are doing it, when you revise your fast-writing, you might think a little more about how to end the lines of your draft.

End-stopping is one method of lineation, and it's very easy to do: simply end lines at places where a person would naturally pause—at the ends of phrases, clauses, sentences. This poem by Jennifer Whitney is a good example:

Post Card BC-2

Bryson City High School turned up in a shoe box
in booth #23 of the Little River Antique Mall.
I thought I had stumbled across Acree Elementary,
my school in Elkhart, Indiana,
years ago. The buildings are almost identical:
imposing brick facades with windows six panes high.
Inside, under twelve foot ceilings,
students sit bent over their desks,
fretting over fractions.

One girl, just like me,
brushes her hair away from her cheek
and pulls her arm free from the notebook page
sticky with sweat. She drowses as the teacher
pecks at the blackboard
with a stubby piece of chalk.
She dreams of high school and boyfriends
who will give her candy in heart-shaped boxes
every February, and flowers in April.
She dreams of being a housewife and mother
who rummages in junk shops,
for curios, like tarnished earrings
or tin pencil boxes
or dingy and yellow postcards in a shoe box.
From that box she will pull one card
and hold it up like a mirror
to see she has not wandered very far in her life.

—Jennifer Whitney

You will notice that many of the lines end with a mark of punctuation, an obvious pause that a reader would make in the sentences. Other lines end at pauses in the phrasing not marked by punctuation. Only one line ends in the middle of a phrase—between the subject and verb: "teacher / pecks."

Read this poem aloud to someone, giving a bit of a pause at the end of each line. (Be careful. Don't pause so long that your listener loses the sense of what the poet is saying.)

Now have your listener read the poem to you. The two of you might talk a bit about why you think the poet ended the lines the way she did.

For practice, revise one or two of the drafts you've written, following the cadences of speech and breaking the lines where a person would naturally pause while reading. Have someone else read your draft to find out how your end-stopped line breaks affect a reader.

4

The Family

My grandmother was the storyteller of the family. When I think of her, I remember the little cabin on the west bluff of the Tennessee River we visited several times a year. After supper, when my sister and I began to fight sleep, GrandSally would sit between us on the dark porch overlooking the river. We would watch the barge lights sweep upstream, and hear fog horns warn other boats of their approach. In this eerie atmosphere, GrandSally would stare out into the night and tell about the ghost that hovered over the cemetery at Bible Hill, and the little girl, Katie, who sat home alone and listened to a black panther scream from the roof. On nights too hot to sleep, she would weave winter tales cold enough to make us shiver. One night she woke my grandfather from a terrible dream. His nightmare had him trapped in Wolf River Cave. It was then he heard a cow in the pasture stuck with calf, and he dressed to help her birth it safely in the frozen grass. As a boy, I longed to be my father growing up in those times. As a grandson and a writer, I owe a debt to GrandSally for her rich stories. I have retold many of them in poems. Sometimes I am the speaker, and sometimes GrandSally is; but in a number of the poems the persona is another member of the family—father, sister, uncle. As I write I see the experience from the point of view of my speaker, and in the process I learn much about how I feel toward my father, his family, and myself.

Some of the most powerful, moving poems, old and new, are about family. We feel our strongest emotions, from anger to love, for those closest to us. Often these poems take the shape of stories, events, or personal reflections. It is in the act of telling that we discover how we feel. Even though the narrators in the following poems are speaking about members of their families, the poems seem to be

directed to a general audience. Read each one as if you were the
persona in the act of telling.

That Morning

That morning in the dark
I tripped on frozen hoof prints
all the way toward the blaring bulb
hanging in the barn and rubbing
sleep from my eyes
saw the birth-wet calf
my father saved.
With her eyes wide open despite the glare,
the mother licked its matted fur,
still steaming from the cold.
We smelled breakfast before it was ready
and long before we were ready to eat.
My father couldn't take his
eyes off the calf. Staring in disbelief,
he told me about his night dream
of being upside down in Wolf River Cave,
how his feet and shoulders seemed
bound in the opposite direction,
and struggling, he had awakened Mother
and she had shook him up.
It was then that he had heard
Melissa lowing in the pasture.
When he got there with a light
all he could see was the back
of a calf, stuck.

He reached his hand all the way
up to find its head and
turned the calf around in the mother's well,
all the time wondering if he
had broken the neck
and then she dropped it in
his lap like a present.
It was a story that had to be
told before he washed the caked
blood from his hands and signaled
for breakfast.

—B. B.

MEMBERS OF THE FAMILY—NOW . . .

One of the simplest ways of writing a poem about a member of the family is to relate an observation of someone close to you. Notice that in the following poem the speaker, a father, tells about his daughter struggling with her writing. In the midst of his observation, he recalls an experience the two of them shared. This past event, related as a flashback, is clearly parallel to the present. At the close of the poem he brings the events together as he sympathizes with her in her struggle.

The Writer

In her room at the prow of the house
Where light breaks, and the windows are tossed with linden,
My daughter is writing a story.

I pause in the stairwell, hearing
From her shut door a commotion of typewriter-keys
Like a chain hauled over a gunwale.

Young as she is, the stuff
Of her life is a great cargo, and some of it heavy:
I wish her a lucky passage.

But now it is she who pauses,
As if to reject my thought and its easy figure.
A stillness greatens, in which

The whole house seems to be thinking,
And then she is at it again with a bunched clamor
Of strokes, and again is silent.

I remember the dazed starling
Which was trapped in that very room, two years ago;
How we stole in, lifted a sash

And retreated, not to affright it;
And how for a helpless hour, through the crack of the door,
We watched the sleek, wild, dark

And iridescent creature
Batter against the brilliance, drop like a glove
To the hard floor, or the desk-top,

And wait then, humped and bloody,
For the wits to try it again; and how our spirits
Rose when, suddenly sure,

It lifted off from a chair-back,
Beating a smooth course for the right window
And clearing the sill of the world.

It is always a matter, my darling,
Of life or death, as I had forgotten. I wish
what I wished you before, but harder.

—Richard Wilbur

Here is a poem in which a son speaks of his father:

White Skies
   (*for my father*)

Mostly, it was the silent frost on the windows
and the soft vision of snow outside
that would hold our questions in.
We had no need to wait for answers;
we could tell from Momma's clenched teeth
when she squatted down familiarly
to stroke the hot-bedded coals.
Father wasn't coming home, and those days
grew flat and stale with waiting.
For a long time I couldn't understand,
but when that last letter came suddenly,
I realized why he stayed away.
Somehow it was easier to know
why Momma slept in an empty bed,
and why my father did not want to impose the agony
of his sickness, or to die
except as a memory frozen beneath the cold,
white skies of home.

—Barry Gilmore

Think of an event or situation about a member of your family. Use details and images to help your reader see the setting and the actions of the incident. What people do reveals a great deal about who they are. Be as personal as you wish, but direct this writing to an outside audience. You'll learn what you have to say as you go. It is in the act of telling that you will discover how you feel.

. . . AND THEN

You might try imagining a close relative in an imagined situation, perhaps a time and situation when you couldn't possibly have been there, as in these two poems:

Confirmation

It's that first moment when you realize
   your mother existed before you were born;
She was herself, without you, unlined eyes,
   hair in rollers. Then you are torn
between love and hating her for being
   suddenly more than lullabyes and first bras,
hating her for changing to more than the ring
   of arms that held you to what she was

Then you see her hands reflected over the sink
   and know that familiar fingers smooth frown lines
      while
you close your eyes, trying to think
   when you first saw creases by her smile.
And you can feel her staring as you sit on cold tile and
      wish
you were six and your doubts still faded with her kiss.

—Katye McCullough

Spider
   —for my father

There were hot summer nights in Chattanooga
when the clubs were so dark
all you could see was a brass horn
shining from the stage.
The man's black cheeks glistened from the shadows
with sweat. They would swell out tight
like a bullfrog. Swell so far
they could almost pop
on the next note,
burst out with his dancing song.
That's when you must have decided
to play the trumpet.
You were skinny and tall,
in the pictures I've seen,
a little awkward. Friends called you Spider.

Those nights you would hang over your chair
and watch how the black man leaned,
his back arched,
trumpet to heaven.
He'd thrust himself deep into the rhythm.

Notes climbed higher and higher
screeching rough but sweet at the top,
and caught the club in a fierce embrace.
You were 15 then,
dreams hung thick in the air.
Now you're 50 and it's Autumn
and the wind blows clear and cool.
You and your band play
for a Thanksgiving crowd.
This is Big Band, soft and swinging,
a hobby away from your music school.
I watch your arms rise with the rhythm
the baton clasped gently in your hand.
I can't see Spider
lingering in your soft limbs
padded with a jacket and tie.
I wonder at the way
summers fade so quickly from memory
with the cold; how hard it is to imagine
the season gone or to come.
Today there is only your music
floating on the cool November air
and the fall leaves blowing
light along the ground.

—Scholle Sawyer

TALKING TO SOMEONE

Family Reunion

My hands, of their own accord, twist
the short brown yarn of the carpet,
make mole-hills in the living room
by pulling one strand, then another.
It gives me something to do
instead of watching you.

Because it's funny how one pause in conversation
about kids, the weather, (nothing, really),
one pause can create this whole silence.
And I can feel it in this room, in my mind,
as I grope for something, anything to say
to break the spell of closed mouths
that I hope don't conceal closed hearts.
Because you're my family, and what am I
supposed to do now that we're all sitting here
acting like strangers? And what would you do
if I stood up and screamed
that I need you and I know that you have problems too.
Your lives can't be full of coffee and the weather,
and old vacations. But I'm still staring at the carpet,
too much like you for my own good.

—Eleanor Womack

Even though most poems assume a larger audience, some directly address a specific person or group. These poems often take the form of letters never sent—what we imagine saying and never do—like the poem "Family Reunion." Sometimes they are spoken to a person, as in the following poem:

March 21st, 1987
   —for Mom's 41st birthday

I've been buying you presents
on your birthday for as many
years as I can remember.
With your money.
Presents that mean nothing to me.
They usually hang in the back of your
closet or rest somewhere in a drawer
or gather dust on the bookshelf
that is stuck way back in the corner
of the attic.
But the squeal of delight when
you unwrap it
(if I've bothered to)
tells me how much it means to you.
I wonder what you thought about me
on your 23rd birthday
when I sat in your womb

and you sat in a hospital bed
opening gifts from Dad
and Grandma and Grandpa.
Were you hoping someone would place
a bow on your stomach so
you would be justified in
opening yourself?
Or were you content to feed me
birthday cake and laugh when I
kicked because it wasn't enough?
I'm glad I waited six days to surprise you
so that your memory of me
would not be mixed with
the perfumes and the clothes
that have been my
gifts to you.

—Dallas Mayberry

All of these poems are saying something to someone on paper that might be hard to say face-to-face. Writing the poem gives you a chance to express those important words, those things you need to say, but never have. Write it down as though you are talking directly to the person.

NOTES AND APOLOGIES

This Is Just to Say

I have eaten
the plums
that were in
the icebox

and which
you were probably
saving
for breakfast

Forgive me
they were delicious
so sweet
and so cold

—William Carlos Williams

This poem appears to be a simple note left on a refrigerator, apologizing for eating someone's plums. I smile every time I read it because I have secretly eaten the last piece of pizza, the last helping of butternut crunch ice cream, and numerous other delectables. All of us are guilty of small crimes like this.

Less Than an Apple
—for Clay

You slammed the front door
on my villainy and
sitting at your piano
played "Rhapsody In Blue"
loud enough to drown out
the fearful cries
of baby ducks I fed
to my boa constrictor
when I couldn't catch mice.

That night you heard
their little peeping
and dreamed the snake
lying still, its cold
eyes motionless,
the only movement
the forked tongue
that jabbed out to the
bluesy rhythm of
Gershwin's music
and when it struck
like a dumb fist
at soft feathers,
you would wake up crying
in your safe bed.

I told you to watch
the snake feed—
grab and swallow up
the head first and then
the webbed feet,
watch the scaley muscles
row the dead lump home
so that your dreams
would not have Eve's curse
crawl out of your closet
offering less than an apple.

> Although this happened
> twenty years ago, Dear Sister,
> this is the story you never tell on me,
> the one you could not forgive.
>
> —B. B.

For whatever reason, all of us have committed acts that seemed almost beyond forgiveness. Since most of our closest emotional ties are with our relatives, it is within the family that we often have our most poignant experiences with guilt and forgiveness. Find your own. Keeping the person you have harmed in mind, write as if you were sending this confession as a letter. It can be funny or serious, but be specific about your crime. Make the details and actions of the event vivid and real. It's all right to change some of the details as long as your poem is still believable. Stay true to the emotions you can feel or conjure up; but suggest them, rather than explaining or stating them directly.

Heavyweight

You were more than my cousin.
No one could throw spirals, bait lines,
or tell jokes like you.
At school they called me names:
fatso, lardo, porky.
But I didn't cry,
you were my friend not theirs.

That October Saturday still feels
crisp and clear.
In your dad's white pickup,
my back to the cab, facing you,
I closed my eyes and listened
to gravel pop under the tires,
and the rhythm you
    tapped on a rusty gas can.

You must have seen my confidence,
the joy of being one year older,
closer to the teenage maturity
which you possessed.

When the rhythm stopped, you said it.
"You're nothing but a fat little boy."

Suddenly the truck bed seemed longer.
Your words crossed that distance,
stinging like yellow jackets
roused by my father's mower.
Damp baking soda couldn't ease this pain.

I realize now, you wanted to shock me,
to make me more than who I was.
I'm thin now
but that fat never left me.
It remains within,
its weight still pulls me down.

—Van Ingram

Words are a powerful force. All of us have been cut to the quick by them. Often we are even hurt by what is not said. In "Heavyweight," a student searched his past for an apology he never received. What he found is still painful. That crisp October Saturday will never leave him. Find an event of your own. Often, anger and hurt are best expressed in quiet ways like the weight that "still pulls me down."

FILM IT

When you are writing about actual events full of emotion, you can often remember quite easily the details of the experience—"the satin black piano," "the ring of arms that held you," the "gravel pop[ping] under the tires." But sometimes you may be writing about memories so far in the past that they seem fuzzy and hard to remember, or you may be creating scenes the way Scholle Sawyer did when she imagined her father as a young man playing his trumpet.

No matter what you are writing about, it is important to see everything clearly in your head; otherwise you won't be able to tell the event so that your reader can see it clearly. This is called "filming it." Before you write, or as you get your words down on paper, recall the experience in your mind: touch, taste, smell, hear, and see the "hot-bedded coals," the "bunched clamor / Of strokes" as someone types, "Gracie's chess pies / steaming on the hutch," "frozen skin against your hat," hands twisting "the short brown yarn of the carpet."

Write down these sense impressions in a few brief words. There is no need to overdress them with a lot of fancy descriptive modifiers. Keep it simple. Then as you draft and rewrite your poem, set down in words the sights, sounds, and smells of that event as you see it running through your mind like a film.

SPEAKING FOR SOMEONE

Poets often assume other personae to narrate first person accounts. In "That Morning" (see the beginning of this chapter) the persona is the poet's father. In the following two poems, students have used the imagined voices of their mothers. In "Defining Terms," Tam Spielman speaks to her infant self through her mother's persona. She isn't telling the reader about her mother; she is letting her audience hear her mother speak. Eleanor Womack's poem, "Garden Legacy," tells a story in her mother's voice. Even though it is about her mother and her baby brother tending a garden, it also reveals something very important about the memory of her father.

Defining Terms
(in my mother's voice)

You are heavy upon my back,
like a sack of potatoes.
As I weed the garden,
pick the green bananas
from the stalk in front
to store under the house
until they fade yellow
in the warm Hawaii twilight,
your weight constantly reminds me
I have a child.
Sometimes in the night
I wake afraid it is
only some firm dream—
the 36-hour labor, the sharp birth pains
almost Caesarean, then your
wide, bright eyes warming me
like the Pacific currents you play in.
I like to think how similar we are—
both allergic to the same pink-white
tree blossoms of the plumeria,
both growing closer until
I think maybe we will be one again.
I will send you to preschool
though I could be your playmate forever—
some day you will be grown
and my term will really end.
Then when you drift
from me it will be your own motion

which will carry you,
and though my muscles
will tighten, I will be still.
These pains are deeper, quieter,
emptier but just as natural.
For a while longer
you will let me carry you
strapped to my back as I work.
I can feel you
growing heavier every day.

—Tamarie Spielman

Garden Legacy

together we bump the car
over the late June grass and dirt road,
bring it to a halt under a tall oak.
You practically jump from the car,
dragging your blanket and "Tommy Tippee" cup
behind you. Your hair grows blond
in the afternoon sun, just like your father's did,
as you run out onto our piece of farm land.
It was the last thing he bought, sort of a legacy
    I guess.
His way of holding on to childhood dreams.
The sun feels so good, so healing on me too
and I sink my knees into the soft, warm earth,
tell you that these are bean plants,
remember when we planted the seeds?
I dig my toes in and yank weeds with a vengeance,
and you follow me, giving each plant
a little of your chocolate milk.
Even the dandelions that I detest so much.

—Eleanor Womack

All of us tell other people's jokes and stories as if they were our own. Often, we use similar gestures and embellishments. It is important that you *try* both approaches to this assignment.

1. In Tam's poem the persona is her mother speaking to Tam as an infant. Assume the voice of a family member and speak for her or

him. Have your speaker talk about something like turning forty, applying for a new job, or having a baby.

2. "Garden Legacy" narrates a story. The persona speaks for the two participants, herself and the little boy. Even though it includes the child, I get the impression that she is thinking this to herself. Think about an event or story in someone else's inner voice.

GRIEVING FOR SOMEONE

When I began teaching creative writing, I steered students away from the topic of death. I felt uncomfortable dealing in class with a subject as personal as grief, my own or others. But, however careful I was to avoid it, death's ugly head kept surfacing in student writing. It began to seem inevitable, necessary. Often these poems were honest, powerful tributes to family and friends, and class members responded with care and respect. Today, I don't avoid death; I confront it in my writing class. My students don't seem to be any more afraid of the subject than I am. Here are three poems about death that show courage and sensitivity.

Eulogy for My Father

Dog Hollow is a long way
from us now.
I remember holding your hand
so bravely
as we walked
right beside Aunt Becker's big, black bull.
Your hands sweated.
I never liked that,
until now.
The wind was cool,
teasing us with its icy fingers.
You saw me shiver
and off came that army jacket
from Vietnam,
full of holes.
It smelled like you.
I remember running my fingers
over the patches
that told what rank you were.
To this day, I still don't know.

But then it didn't matter.
I leaned over to hug
you so you wouldn't freeze.
Seven years passed . . .
sitting in an orange chair
beside your bed,
invaded by those antiseptic smells.
I was shivering.
You saw me.
I found your army jacket
two days after you had gone
and put on
what was left.

—Tiffany Thurman

Aunt Clara's Flight

I never could cry right
when somebody died
the tears would come out,
the feeling in my stomach
was always there,
but I didn't know enough
I didn't know how death felt
how it looked
why it was
nobody knew
nobody could tell me
if they did

Aunt Clara died

and all they could say
was
"she's gone"
gone where?
no one said

I went to her house
she wasn't there

I wanted to ask her
I wanted her to explain
why she had to go

but I couldn't find her

when mama found me
crying beside the porch
she said

"Aunt Clara's up there"

she pointed at the sky

but I couldn't see her
because
the sun was in the way.

—Jerel Walden

April Fool

You were more of a father
to other boys. I hated
machines and couldn't put
up a tight tent.
You liked me most when I played
first string guard or was fast
and mean in Golden Gloves.
I quit the year you died.
I still brag sometimes
about nosing up to players
fifty pounds heavier, meeting
them head on.
I say this as if I were you
forgetting this is a conversation
I would never start.
I am thirty-six and once a year I still
celebrate my grief.
This year I was standing at the counter
of a roadside market
when a lady asked, "Is today the thirty-first?"
and the date caught
in my throat.
At 8:07 p.m., March 31, 1964,
you clutched your heart.
And even though your pulse was gone
I gave you mouth-to-mouth.
I had to do something
with my terror

and your beard stubble rubbed my mouth raw
for forty minutes before the doctor came.
At the funeral my nose and cheeks still burned.
Everyone thought they were signs of grief–they
      were,
the grief you understood.

—B. B.

Writing about someone's death, whether the person is close to you or not, is a personal, even intimate, experience. You should find your own way to eulogize or grieve. You might follow the lead of one of the poems in this section. Even if your approach to this subject is similar to another writer's when you begin, you will soon find that your writing takes you in new directions, to your own way of expressing your experience.

Whatever the tone of your piece, it is best to keep your writing honest. In writing, the word *honest* doesn't just mean the truth, but how the truth is told. If the poet is trying to impress the reader with his or her pompous style, the truth of the emotion will be lost. Reread the poem "April Fool." The speaker is a grown man who is telling his dead father what he couldn't say earlier, a message he has grown to realize. He opens with, "You were more of a father / to other boys." At the very beginning he expresses an honest and painful message.

Later in "April Fool" the son reveals the details of his father's death and how he tried to save him. "And even though your pulse was gone / I gave you mouth-to-mouth. / I had to do something / with my terror / and your beard stubble rubbed my mouth raw . . . " The specific details described in this failed rescue empower the poem with emotion. Enrich your poems with sensual images, descriptions that ask your reader to see, feel, smell, and hear. Be specific.

It is also important to let the facts of your experience speak for themselves. You don't need to tell or explain how you felt with abstractions like *sad* or *painful*. Concrete details validate the events you relate and make convincing the emotional truth the experience implies. It is better to understate than overstate and run the danger of becoming sentimental. Understating is an effective way of expressing powerful and intensely personal emotions. Trust your readers to feel emotions on their own.

Millie

The sun is shining
      it is spring and

                                        today we buried Millie.
                    We toss our fistfuls of dirt
                                leave the cemetery
                                        and walk to the junkyard.
                    Her car sits demolished
                                on a flat-bed truck.
                    We climb and search
                                among congealed blood and shattered glass
                                        for the last moments of Millie's life.
                    Getting down we shake the car and
                                blood trickles
                                        onto the rusty surface of the truck.
                    We stare, silent
                                until the dripping stops.
                    Louise pulls a Kleenex
                                from her purse and
                                        soaks up her sister's blood
                                                then returns it to her purse and
                                        snaps it closed.

                                                        —Vicki Chezem

Notice how effectively Vicki uses an understated tone in her poem. By saying less than she might, she trusts the reader to respond to the event as she did. After all, when she made her visit to the junkyard, she had no one standing there to *tell* her she should feel sad. Her emotional reaction was inevitable given the facts of the experience. She *shows* us what it was like to live through this brief part of her life and then leaves us to respond in our own way. The details and actions she presents won't allow us to come away from this poem feeling overjoyed; they lead us inevitably to feel sadness and shock—just as Vicki did.

ENJAMBING

Weeding Crabgrass

While kneeling in the shade
of my hat, digging out the crabgrass
which has spread like a plague
of starfish, I recall
my mother. "Half an hour working   5

in the yard," she would say, "and then
you can go swimming." Easy time
to do, I thought—the first
time. But the minutes multiplied
to hours under the slow baking   10
sun of high June. In moments my fingers
were ragged earth-grubbers, nails
torn and dirt-blackened beyond the power
of the swimming pool to cleanse.

I sat cross-legged, the grass bristling   15
against my skin, and watched my patch
of weedless lawn grow—but far
too slowly. A half hour made so small
a dent in the blaze of weeds across
the earth.
               I have come to understand   20
that weeding is power, our small attempt
to make sense of our having been
here, shaping the world our way.

But when I stand, across the green   25
sky, I see constellations beyond reason.

               —Jennifer Whitney

In chapter 3 you learned about end-stopping, breaking lines at natural pauses in sense and syntax. Are there any such line breaks in "Weeding Crabgrass"? There may be a couple of places—between lines 2 and 3, 5 and 6, 20 and 21. Most of the time, though, the lines of this poem end in the middle of phrases, between words you wouldn't expect to find separated, like a subject and its verb ("fingers / were") or a verb and its complement ("recall / my mother"). Other breaks separate nouns and their qualifiers: "first / time," "baking / sun," "nails / torn," and "patch / of weedless lawn." The breaks often come at exactly the point in the sentence where a reader *wouldn't* pause while reading. This is called "enjambment" or "run-on lines." Poets can create several effects using the technique:

1. Enjambing may emphasize the words at the beginnings or endings of lines. For example, the break between lines 12 and 13 makes both the end and beginning words (*nails / torn*) more noticeable.

2. Sometimes, such line breaks create a tension between words, a little moment of suspense as the reader moves from the last word

on one line to the word beginning the next one. Readers may be in for a bit of surprise when they leave *power* at the end of line 13 and find *of the swimming pool* at the start of the next line, probably not quite what they were expecting. Creating such moments of tension and uncertainty will keep readers just a bit off balance—expectant, surprised.

Read the poem aloud to someone and have that person read it back to you. Let your listener know where the line breaks come by pausing slightly, about a half-comma's worth. As you read, look for other line breaks in the poem where there is a little twist and surprise as you move from one line to the next.

Pull out a draft of a poem you have been working on (or one you haven't looked at in a while) and revise it using enjambment as much as you like. Then read the poem to a reading/listening partner and talk about the effects created by the lineation. The two of you should point out line breaks that are effective—and try to explain why you think they are.

Now help your listening/reading partner do the same with a draft.

PROSE POEMS

Emjambment is an effective way to make a piece of writing seem less prose like; but sometimes narrative poems sound like prose, even when the piece is broken into lines and enjambed. In the following selection I retell a story told me by my brother over Thanksgiving dinner some forty years after the event. Maybe the fact that I heard the story told aloud prompted me to adopt a proselike voice when I wrote it down. Although it sounds like prose and has passages in which I comment on the events (a little bit the way the writer of an essay might do), I can still see elements in my draft that a reader might expect to find in poetry rather than prose—the imagery and metaphors, for example.

At first I tried to enjamb the lines of this piece to make it sing and to give it a movement and rhythm. Finally, I decided it was best to type it as prose. In this format my piece might be called a "prose poem," a kind of poem (or prose?) a good many writers have written.

Silent Hope
(*Clark's childhood memory, 1946*)

When news came my father was returning from war, mother left to meet him on the west coast. Aunt Mary and

J. D. drove me from the Mississippi delta to the Tennessee River hills where my grandparents had me a warm feather bed, a dog-trot for my toys and a sooner hound named Bob.

That night, I stared out the dark window hoping by some miracle to see my mother's small frame, when a truck door slammed and a man's dark shape walked across the porch. A commercial fisherman from Perryville had rammed two large fish hooks in his one good hand, had driven with elbows up the bluff for GrandMilt to cut them out.

Extra lanterns were lit around the kitchen table, while GrandSally boiled thread. The fisherman slowly spread his cramped claw for us to see, one hook buried in the palm, the other in the index finger. My grandfather poured the only whiskey served in the house, a glass for the man and the rest into a washbowl. I watched as he forced the barbs through flesh and skin, clipped them off, then pulled the shafts back out. He lanced the punctures so they would bleed and held the man's hand in the bloody moonshine without a word. GrandSally sewed the wounds, bandaged them with strips of sheet and Milt drove him home. I fell asleep that night awestruck that I had witnessed what I had only heard about from books.

Soon my homesickness eased with days filled with feeding tomato peels to chickens and running the close fields with old Bob. Nights after supper, my dark window showed dreams of my mother's return, her tense smile melted into my father's arms, and I would remember the tight shoulders of that fisherman as he moved toward the silent hope of my grandparents, cradling his good hand in his left arm like a child.

—B. B.

5

Animals

Wags was an arrogant, snotty little dog who disliked uniforms and anyone who wore them. Policemen, mailmen, milk truck drivers, meter maids, Salvation Army bell ringers, and cub scouts—he showed no favoritism. He hated them all. This mutt wouldn't confront uniformed persons directly. He would hide, sneak up behind them, and nip their calves before they knew what got them. Then he'd bound back ten feet and imitate a dwarf tyrannosaurus, propped up on his haunches, lip curled, fangs bared.

Wags was smart too. When he got bored, he'd trot a mile to town to visit my father. He would wait at the door to the business and enter behind the next visitor. The secretary was trained to say, "Wags, Mr. Brown isn't in," and he'd cock his head to show he knew it was a scam and then ramble back home.

Wags was born a week before me and he never let me forget it. He treated me as an inferior, the same as my older brothers and sister did. Even my mother called his name before mine when she summoned us home for supper. Every time his name comes up at holiday gatherings, my family remembers this sibling pecking order with great relish.

I don't know whether I actually remember experiencing these stories, or whether I retell them as an important part of family history, "The Wags Era." All I know is that when I was nine, a handyman, trying to keep Wags out of the basement, accidentally slammed the door on his head and killed him. It is rumored that Clark got the rifle out of my father's closet to shoot the poor guy, and my oldest brother stopped him.

Poets write about favorite pets because they are an important part of our personal histories. The following poems differ in many ways.

Some tell events and others describe actions and personalities. Some are narrated in first person and some in third. In all of them it is clear that the speakers care about the subject and know the specific habits of the animals well.

How It Began

They struggled their legs and blindly loved, those puppies
inside my jacket as I walked through town. They crawled
for warmth and licked each other—their poor mother
dead, and one kind boy to save them. I spread
my arms over their world and hurried along.

At Ellen's place I knocked and waited—the tumult
invading my sleeves, all my jacket alive.
When she came to the door we tumbled—black, white,
gray, hungry—all over the living room floor
together, rolling, whining, happy and blind.

—William Stafford

Cat Nap

Ming sits
on my bed and
nudges me enough to
make me stop and pet her,
but the break is nice.
I've lost my train of thought
and imagine Ming,
a black panther,
slinking in the shadows
of a wet jungle
still dripping from
a recent rain.
She hides in the shadow
of a banana tree
with only her yellow
eyes reflecting the watering
gazelle that is unaware
of its ardent admirer.
Ming dares to move and
the gazelle lifts its head
and listens.

Ming freezes.
The gazelle, now
comfortable, takes another
long drink and sensing this,
Ming springs forward
at the butterfly but misses
and she sits sheepishly
on my bed sheet and I
go back to my biology.

—Gina Gardner

Blues for Old Dogs

It's summer and the dogs decline in heat,
A time again for four letter words,
Gout, tick, mite, flea and worm.
Zimmer's dogs moan and flay themselves,
Tossing heads till their ears crack.
They dribble, pump, loll their tongues.
At night, old dreams return like storms
That roam the world and come each summer
To make them tremble and dash in sleep.
These days Zimmer is a sad mutt, too.
Sometimes when the moon rises
He lays down his rancid, aging body
And says, Dear Friends, come let us
Sing a little groaning song together.

—Paul Zimmer

The Hermit Meets the Skunk

The hermit's dog skitters home
drunk with it once every fall,
the whites of his eyes marbled
from the spray and his tail tucked
tighter than a clamshell. He contracts
himself to a mouse under the hermit's bed.

The hermit unsticks him with a broom
and ties him outside to a tree.
He is a spotted dog, black rampant
on white. And as the hermit scrubs,
the white goes satiny with Lava soap,
the black brightens to a bootblack shine.

Next, a dose of tomato juice stains
the white like a razor cut under water
and purples the black, and after that
the whole dog bleaches mooncolored
under a drench of cornstarch.
The hermit sniffs him. Skunk
is still plain as a train announcement.

So he is to be washed again,
rinsed again, powdered again
until the spots wink out again
under the neutral white.
Inside his mouth, the hermit knows
and knows from what is visible
under the tail, Dog is equally spotted
but in the interior, grey on a pink field.
If he were to be pinned down,
his four legs held at four corners,
and slit open by the enthusiast,
the hermit knows the true nature of Dog
spotted layer by layer
would be laid bare.

Afterward all night
skunk sleepwalks the house.
Skunk is a pot of copper pennies
scorched dry on a high flame.
Skunk is a porridge of dead shrews
stewed down to gelatin.
Skunk is the bloat of chicken gut
left ten days to sweeten in the sun.
Skunk is the mother bed, the ripe taste
of carrion, the green kiss.

                              —Maxine Kumin

    Think about your present or past pets. Remember any stories like
the arrival of the pet, the day the cat strutted in and dropped a dead
mole on the kitchen table, or when the gerbil got loose and made a
nest in one of your father's best shoes. You might start with a peculiar
habit like "the old dog winking a half-opened sleepy eye." Or an
action, like "They struggled their legs."

THE WILD OUTDOORS

The Crows

I shortcut home between Wade's tipsy shocks,
And lookout crows alert in the bare elm
Ask each other about this form that walks
Stubbled mud they considered their own farm.
They know there's death and loss where such shapes go.
I have no gun—I even feel akin
To these rude, lively birds. But to a crow
Kinship means Crow, and I'm not of his clan.

Off they flap to the wood with a hoarse curse,
And though the landscape's greyer with them gone
I'm glad they're skeptics—someday someone else
Trudging these ruts may raise a sudden gun.
Distrust me, crow!—the not-as-crow—, the other.
Croak, 'Damn your eyes!', and call no man your brother.

—Leah Bodine Drake

In "The Crows" the narrator feels a kinship to these "lively birds," but both know that she's not of the crow clan. Although the speaker means them no harm, their mistrust might one day save them from men with guns. All of us, city and country dwellers alike, encounter wild animals, from the squirrels in the yard and pigeons on the roof to the spiders in the shadowy corners of our bedrooms. The next poems come from a variety of settings: cities, farms, and the wilderness. Each involves a personal encounter with an animal. Notice how the writers of these poems help the reader see their subjects through vivid images and closely observed details.

For Brook Trout in Sky Top Creek

I whip the fly rod
through the air
until the fly comes
to rest upon the creek surface
and I sit upon my rock
and watch the current
take it, whipping it
away from the white water
toward the dark shadows below
and then I see the

slight twitch of the line
and I lift up quickly
until I feel your pull
against mine and see the sunlight
through the water on your back
I bring you in closer
to me in shallow water
and bend down and draw you up
into my hands, into the breeze
You struggle until I turn you
back down, belly up
and I can feel you breathing
You would have me think
that some oriental painter
wandered to these waters
and dappled upon your scales—
wonder why you do not hang
in the Freer Gallery
among the other water colors—
but I know as I unhook you
your colors will not wash off
if I toss you back
perhaps the water will soak you up
I throw you gently into the air
almost expecting you to find
your way in it—
you fall, your scales rippling
and swim away to the rocks
deep beneath
the sunshine—
a dark shadow

—Tamarie Spielman

A Damnation of Doves

Where did doves perch before there were telephone wires?
I think they evolved in cemeteries. The dead
might tolerate them; they don't have to hear
that coo dripping forever. Mohammud said
Noah's dove is in Heaven, one of the ten
creature-saints so honored in the Koran

for having done God's will. But tell me how
it managed to break that twig from the olive tree.

What did it use for pruning shears? I know
it was miracle time back there in deep B.C.,
but who would have been offended had a hawk
with a proper cutting beak been assigned the work?

Were there a hawk in Heaven, I'd pray it down
to feed on doves. That wouldn't interfere
with the balance of nature. And once the work was done
I might manage to rinse this *coo!-coo!* from my ears
by singing hymns, or by kneeling to TV,
or whatever does for ritual in A.D.

—John Ciardi

Turkey Story

We stopped the truck on Rafter Road
to greet a young turkey homeless,
motherless. It chattered to you
in bird and poked its head like a
periscope in WW II movies firing
at you, its new mother. I said
with two ten-year-old tomcats
at home, what can we do with
a wild turkey, but as if it
knew impracticality
it rushed into the
mountain brush,
coyote-raccoon-
fox-bobcat brush,
this fluff-headed
butterball, mother-
less, hunting the
perfect mother
of us
all.

—B. B.

Brainstorm a list of animals you have encountered in the past. If
you have memories of zoo or farm animals, include those. Remember
the colors and textures of fur, feathers, scales, or skin. Can these
textures be compared to other things you know, such as orchard
grass, snow flakes, maple bark, or marble? Figurative comparisons of
this kind not only give your reader a more accurate description, they
also bring into the poem connotations associated with the secondary

image. Comparing the turkey's swivelling head to a periscope brings into the poem connotations of the mechanical motions of that secondary image, possibly suggestions of sneakiness, too. Narrate your experience with the animal and feel free to speak directly to it.

WILD VOICES

One spring morning my sister and I awoke to find that the big black cat we named Tom had given birth to seven mousy kittens. Imagine my mother's surprise to find them snug in a box of old sweaters in our closet. They were like wiggling, furry beanbags. If this feline mother of seven could have spoken, she might have said, "Listen, name me Midnight, Martha, or Gypsy, but not Tom."

Have you ever wondered what your pet would say if it could talk? In the next two poems, the poets assume their pets' voices and speak for them. "Winterpig" is from a series of poems Denise Levertov wrote about a pet pig.

Winterpig

At the quick of winter
moonbrightest
snowdeepest

we would set out.
I'd run up my ramp
into the pickup,

we'd rattle and shake
two midnight miles
to the right hill.

Then on foot,
slither and struggle
up it—

they'd
ready their sled
and toboggan down

and I'd
put down my nose and
spread my ears and

tear down beside them,
fountains of snow
spurting around me:

I and my Humans
shouting, grunting,
the three of us

wild with joy,
just missing
the huge maples.

Yes, over and over
up to the top of the
diamond hill—

the leanest, the fastest,
most snow-and-moon-and-midnight-bewitched
pig in the world!

—Denise Levertov

Cindy Damon's poem, "The Age of a Golden," is an emulation of Denise Levertov's. Damon uses several of Levertov's titles to get her started. Through these brief monologues, Guinevere, Cindy's golden retriever, reveals her personality and her relationship to her owner and mistress. Here are several sections from her poem:

The Age of a Golden
III   My delight

I show her
joy in snowwiggles
glorious angels from
whiskered-halo to
sweeping tail-wing
ecstatic snowdiving rolls
we frolic
and churn snowshowers
for buried balls

IV   My gift

I sniff out treasures
ripe socks and
underpants

I offer these
to our guests' laps
in welcome

along sidewalks I
discover secret scents
delight in signatures
and potent presents
answer Her anger
with lowered head.

VII   My demand

Near five
like clockwork
I do my dinner dance
toenails clicking
insistently
beside empty bowl
I prance back and forth
urgently wagging
beseech her
yodel high
and low, serenade
her for my supper

—Cindy Damon

You can have your pet, or any animal you know well, tell its own story, as Cindy did. It can be divided into a series of short pieces, but it doesn't have to be. It could be about a kitten getting stuck in a tree or a dog stretched out in front of a radiator dreaming about spring. Try to capture the personality of your animal through its voice and experiences.

CUTTING WORDS

Good writing is descriptive, but many people think the word *descriptive* means using qualifiers—adjectives and adverbs. And beginning writers often think the more, the better:

Barbara smiled cheerily at the lonely little sloth—shaggy-haired and bow-legged—which was walking slowly and dejectedly toward her with a sad, hangdog expression on its face.

This sentence is heavy with adjectives and adverbs. Try cutting it to about ten to fifteen words. Don't cut articles and connecting words, just unneeded qualifiers. For each group of two or three qualifiers in this sentence, come up with the best *one*, or a good one of your own. Try to get rid of language that is

1. redundant (saying the same thing twice): "It was a recurring nightmare that kept happening over and over."
2. abstract (stating emotions or ideas rather than letting images imply them): instead of saying "the trout was beautiful," you could say, as Tam did in "For Brook Trout in Sky Top Creek," "some painter / . . . dappled upon your scales."
3. commonplace or trite (using worn-out or conventional images or comparisons): "The clouds looked like cotton balls."
4. self-consciously fancy diction (using phony or pretentious words): "The azure, somnolent ocean enveloped me totally with its soporific susurration."

And keep in mind that you don't have to describe *everything* about your subject all in one sentence; you might refer to the sloth's loneliness somewhere else in your poem.

Poetry is economical and compressed. Most of the time poets get more mileage out of fewer words than prose writers do. The power and sharpness of your writing has little to do with the size of your vocabulary. It is more important to use with precision the words you already know and are familiar with.

Instead of a string of qualifiers that bogs the reader down and turns your style to soggy mash potatoes, be specific; give your reader lean meat—particular nouns (instead of *tree,* say *sycamore*) and active verbs (*tumble, prance, clip, dash, slither*).

Find someone in your class whom you've never worked with before and get together with several drafts of poems in hand. Try one or several of these exercises:

1. Read one of your drafts aloud to your coworker; then have him or her do the same. Listen for words or phrases that could be cut.
2. Read one of your friend's drafts aloud; both of you listen for words to delete for stronger and more economical writing.
3. Swap drafts you haven't read to each other before. Mark suggested cuts on your friend's draft, have your friend do the same to yours.

IN THE FIELDS OF DEATH

Drought

Our dog tried to have puppies
too big for such a small dog,
so we took her to a shade-tree vet,
who sliced her open with a razor blade.
Wet, black bodies spilled out
like olives onto a white tablecloth.
I couldn't decide whether to cry or laugh.
He sewed her up, said she'd be fine,
and put the puppies in a box.

Dad stopped on a bridge,
took the box from me,
carried it to the edge,
waited to make sure no car came along,
and dropped it.
I leaned so far that he grabbed my arm,
and I counted to eight
before the tiny box
hit the dry creek bed.

—Steven West

Animals' deaths are linked to our experience in many ways. We
raise and kill them to eat. We kill them for sport and out of necessity
because we believe that their presence poses a danger or an inconve-
nience. Sometimes we cause animal deaths accidentally, sometimes
through greed. When we are confronted with suffering animals, we
kill them out of compassion. In the next two poems, the writers
present stories and feelings about killing animals.

Killing the Rattlesnake

At first I thought it was a bullsnake,
its constrictive muscles edging
gravel aside as it "S'd" its way
up the drive. Then the sharp diamond
pattern emerged like a thick ribbon
tapering into the black of rattler.
Damn it, I said. I had to kill it.
I've encountered copperheads and rattlers
in the woods, admired their slick

beautiful patterns. But I could hear
my nieces playing in the yard, could see
the Holmes' boys on their bikes
being circled by dogs. I got the hoe
and came down hard at its head,
missed slicing a deep slash
of ribs and flesh.

It struck like a fist and ground
its mouth against the wooden handle.
Venom showered my feet, streamed
down the wood; it meant to kill
what was killing it.
In my fear, I struck and struck
and struck until it lay quivering
in pieces, executed for a crime
it had only the potential to commit.
The violent chopping brought
a neighborhood of kids who stood
awed by a fear older than the fallen angel.
I felt dirty, unclean.
This made me the hero of that Saturday.

I skinned it, cleaned it in Borax,
rubbed it with Neats foot oil and patched
the pieces together on a board.
I have been compelled to tell this story
over and over to friends who stare
at the crooked diamonds and count rattles.
I catch them scanning the ground when walking
in my yard and I smile, but sometimes
I feel like the kid who has drawn a line
in front of a bully. I still dream
eyes in dark places.

—B. B.

Ode to a Pig

I saw you
sitting in your pen
when you were very small
eating the leftovers
of Thanksgiving dinner.

I think of that now
as I watch you suffer
the degradation
that millions have suffered
before you.
I watch while
Uncle Odie, Fat, and Dad
push you in
the carpet covered bed
of Fat's truck.
I can smell the fear
as you think of the vat that they will
dip your carcass in to remove
the bristles that you were so proud of,
the knife to slice
open your stomach,
the ground that is enriched
by your blood,
and the brine that you
will soak in
like a frog for a biology class.
I watch Fat load the shells
into the shotgun
but I turn away
when he sticks the barrel
to your ear.
The squeal is cut
by the gun's sharp retort.

—Dallas Mayberry

I have been shocked awake in the middle of the night when a
wasp stung me on the cheek. The only regret I had in killing the critter
is that I hadn't done it before the sting made my jaw balloon. I have
stopped to kill a quivering, kicking cat that some car had hit on the
road in the front of my garden. I have directly or indirectly caused the
deaths of many animals. Almost every time I do, I am left with a need
to explain. Maybe it's because of my feelings of remorse, and maybe
it's related to an unexplainable curiosity about death. I have written
many poems about the subject.

Find your own experience. Recapture the event, and let your
telling of the story imply your feelings of sorrow or curiosity, regret
or fear.

FINAL SCENES

Old Dog

Toward the last in the morning she could not
get up, even when I rattled her pan.
I helped her into the yard, but she stumbled
and fell. I knew it was time.

The last night a mist drifted over the fields.
In the morning she would not raise her head—
the far, clear mountains we had walked
surged back to mind.

We looked a slow bargain: our days together
were the ones we had already had.
I gave her something the vet had given,
and patted her still, a good last friend.

—William Stafford

Our pets' life spans are shorter than our own. They live with us
until they die, and we bury them as old friends or family members. In
"Old Dog" and the next two poems, the speakers tell about the events
surrounding the death of aged pet companions.

Dad's Dog

Sally was Dad's
dog, who was older
than I was—
about 15 to my 8

she was old and
frail—
with some kind of
skin disease
(I never knew
exactly what kind—
it never bothered me.)

One Saturday morning,
I got up out of
my loft
and peered out the
window to see

what the weather
was like. I noticed
the leaves blowing
by the chicken
shack, and two
white chickens
that had gotten loose.

I grabbed my pants
and slithered
into them—running
to the chickens,
I neared them
and suddenly slowed.

What had been
chicken necks
were now the 2 white upturned
legs of Sally—

for the first
time in years,
her eyes
free of pain.

—Doug Schatz

Loyal

They gave him an overdose
of anesthetic, and its fog
shut down his heart in seconds.
I tried to hold him, but he was
somewhere else. For so much of love
one of the principals is missing,
it's no wonder we confuse love
with longing. Oh I was thick
with both. I wanted my dog
to live forever and while I was
working on impossibilities
I wanted to live forever, too.
I wanted company and to be alone.
I wanted to know how they trash
a stiff ninety-five-pound dog
and I paid them to do it

and not tell me. What else?
I wanted a letter of apology
delivered by decrepit hand,
by someone shattered for each time
I'd had to eat pure pain. I wanted
to weep, not "like a baby,"
in gulps and breath-stretching
howls, but steadily, like an adult,
according to the fiction
that there is work to be done,
and almost inconsolably.

—William Matthews

In "Dad's Dog," the narrator introduces Sally and related the unusual experience of finding her dead, "for the first time in years, her eyes free of pain." "Loyal" is a personal account about a pet owner who pays a vet to have his old friend put to sleep. The narrator goes on to reveal how he reacted emotionally to the experience. In doing so, he suggests a great deal about himself and his inadequacies in dealing with the situation. These poems are strikingly honest, and they suggest a wide range of emotions. Notice how humor and irony are sometimes mixed with feelings of sadness and regret.

BURIALS

On the dark afternoon of Wags's death, my two older brothers made a wooden box to hold his body. When the grave was deep enough so that the wild animals wouldn't dig him up, the funeral procession started. My family and a few neighborhood kids followed behind my brothers as they led us under the great oak where we gave Wags back to the earth. I could take you there today.

The next three poems are about dead animals being returned to the ground.

Mouse Elegy

After he petted his mouse awhile,
Gabriel said, "He's really still,
he doesn't move at all," running his
small finger over the tiny
luxurious black and white back,
and then in awe and shock he said "He's—

dead." I lifted him out of his cage in his
bed, a brown-rice box, and Gabey
turned and turned his chest as if
struggling to get unstrapped from something,
twisting and twisting from the waist up and then
trying to get ahold of me
several times as if he couldn't, as
if something was holding him by the body but
finally it broke, he came into my arms,
I said whatever you say then,
My darling, my sweetheart.
We got a hanky with roses on it and
laid it on the kitchen floor and laid
Blackie on it. He drifted there like a
long comma,
front paws, pink and tiny as
chips of broken crockery, held
up in wonder, like a shepherd at the Christ Child's
creche; back paws strong as a jackrabbit's
thrust back in mid-leap; and the
thick whisker of the tail arrested in a
lovely male curve. We kneeled on
either side of the miniature head,
wedge-shaped and white, floating there with an
air of calm absence and demanding dreams.
I started to roll up the hanky, rocking the
light body a little, and one of his
ears unfurled, a grey petal
opening slowly in the night, and then we
wrapped Blackie in red roses and
paper towels, Gabe laid him in the glossy
black box lined with crimson
the champagne came in, we put it in the freezer
until we could take him to the country and crack the
frozen ground with axes so Blackie can
lie with the others in the earth, in a field of mice.

—Sharon Olds

The Neighbor's Cat

He's lying underneath
the tree beside my bedroom window
buried in a make-shift grave,

covered with pine needles.
His yellow hairs are gray with ice
and his restless claws
no longer raise the red clay
that surrounds him.
We stand at a distance
staring into his empty eyesockets
with curiosity.
Gaping at his stiff jaw,
mouth still ajar, perhaps poised
for one final curse at us idle onlookers,
or an impatient call for
the snows of winter
that will cover his grave.

—Chris Covington

The Dead Calf

Dead at the pasture edge,
his head is without eyes, becalmed
on the grass. There was no escaping
the heaviness that came on him,
the darkness that rose
under his belly as though he stood
in a black sucking pool.
Earth's weight grew in him,
and he lay down. As he died
a great bird took his eyes.

Where is the horror in it?
Not in him, for he came to it
as a shadow into the night.
It was nameless and familiar.
He was fitted to it. In me
is where the horror is. In my mind
he does not yield. I cannot believe
the deep peace that has come to him.
I am afraid that where the light
is torn there is a wound.
There is a darkness in the soul
that loves the eyes. There is a light
in the mind that sees only light
and will not enter the darkness.

But I would have a darkness
in my mind like the dark
the dead calf makes for a time
on the grass where he lies, and will make
in the earth as he is carried down.
May all dead things lie down in me
and be at peace, as in the ground.

—Wendell Berry

If you have buried a pet, write its funeral poem. You can start with
the story of its death or with the burial. You might compose a eulogy,
perhaps, or a final prayer for any dead animal that you have found or
that you know about.

BACK TO LIFE

Insects, reptiles, fish, birds, and mammals are complex, fascinating
creatures. Some tiny, shy spiders are deadly poisonous and live in our
houses. Some mammals fly at night, carry their young in pouches,
and sleep upside down in caves. There are catfish that crawl out of the
water at night and scavenge on land. Common possums are some of
the oldest living mammals. They give birth to young the size of field
peas. When surprised by humans, they pretend to be dead. I've seen
possums lie on their backs and stick their tongues out the side of their
mouths.

The next poems contain detailed accounts of common animals.
Read them carefully, trying to visualize what you read.

The Southern Brown Recluse

Anything hidden is suspect—
borders of curtains
never opened behind the dresser,
the caverns in old clothes,

toes of old summer shoes
back in the dark, forgotten. Shy,
formal in a brown-velvet hourglass body,
it bears a white guitar on its back,

its only music. Disturbed,
in terror of light, it stings anything
exposed—ankles invading closets,
hands gathering garments

for charity or probing
for lost coins. Its venom
rots the skin. Only at night
will it crawl out, great crab-legs

feeling familiar carpet trails
like a beach strewn with shells
of flies, silver racers,
crickets. Whatever it stalks

tonight will burn
twitching, paralyzed, a string
of live flesh like a trot line.
Later, while the moon glows

through curtains like tapestries,
it will drag its catch
back to the secret fabrics,
reclusive and famished.

All the dark day, its long legs
caress each victim turned to jelly,
even the bones, and then it bends down
its straw tongue like a kiss.

—Walter McDonald

Buzzards

Mornings, a buzzard works alone,
coroner of the country roads.
He works for the state;
he has the right of way.

At noon he plants himself
atop the ruin of an elm,
his wings spread wide,
his necked arched to the sun
as if he were the ornament
on the hood of death's car.
The buzzard is inviting light
into his embrace, as lice
escape from his cloak.

When you see them wheeling
in the air, don't think buzzards
have to wait for carrion—

the country-side is full of it.
Buzzards always take
the afternoon off to soar
on the earth's warm breath
and count their shadows
slipping over the fields.

Their work is easy and can wait.
Buzzards sleep late,
huddled in their cloaks—
in the branches of a locust—
a candelabrum lit with black flames.
When finally they blossom
onto the morning air, the scrape
of their wings in the branches
is the scent they leave.

—David LaMotte

The Vixen
—for Elizabeth Pollack

The vixen,
when she would feed her young,
trots off from the den
in moonlight, crouching
only when she reaches
the mouse-rich field.

What does she know?
that she is a fox? has paws?
a mouth? She never grieves
for hands, some stance in the field
other than her own.

This is her sure place.
One by one, she culls the mice
for her kits, crushes their necks
places them in a ring;
she sees neither sun nor star
where their tails cross in the center.
Were she to speak, she would say
about need and the cooperative moon:
this is how one arranges things.

—Linda McCarriston

These poems contain a lot of information conveyed through imagery and comparison. The brown recluse spider's "venom rots the skin," and buzzards preen their feathers in the sun to rid themselves of lice. The information and descriptive detail are often embellished with figurative comparisons. Whatever the spider stalks "will burn / twitching, paralyzed, / a string of live flesh like a trot line" (simile). "Atop the ruin of an elm," the buzzard is "the ornament / on the hood of death's car" (metaphor). But these are poems, not essays in an encyclopedia. Facts are conveyed to the reader through imagery, simile, and metaphor, rather than through flat expository statements. In poetry (and in much good prose too, for that matter) you can inform *and* surprise—several ways at once.

Choose a creature you're interested in and find out something about its habits—what it eats, when it mates, how it takes care of its young, where and when it sleeps and plays. Put your information aside for a while. Then without looking back at your notes, sit down and write. Trust your memory to give you the most interesting facts. You can check your notes later when you revise—just to be sure.

ADDING WORDS

Cutting unneeded words will strengthen a poem because writing often hits harder when a few words give the reader more experience and emotion than expected. This is what the poet Ezra Pound meant when he said, "Less is more."

But it is also possible to increase the power of your writing by adding words.

The image "the sharp diamond / pattern emerged" is a sharp detail, but the poet makes it even sharper:

> the sharp diamond
> pattern emerged like a thick ribbon
> tapering into the black of rattler.

In that same poem the simile "[the snake] struck like a fist" adds punch to the action. Further on, the abstract word *fear* takes on new life and renewed emotional impact through a simile: "the fear older than the fallen angel."

Writing figurative comparisons like these similes and metaphors is just as easy as it looks, but it will take practice: although everyone uses metaphorical expressions in conversation all the time ("Cut that out!"; "He sat there looking at me like a drooling baby"), most of us aren't used to writing them down.

As a poet your job is to keep writing similes and metaphors so that seeing things figuratively and writing metaphorical images becomes natural to you.

To begin practicing, pull out a draft of one of your poems about animals, since they will probably have good concrete detail. See if you can improve some of your images by adding figurative comparisons.

At first it may seem that your efforts are forced or contrived, but keep at it: the more you write, the more natural your comparisons will become; and in time you will find that you are writing similes and metaphors in early drafts and fast-writings without even thinking about it.

6

Growing Up in the Nuclear Age

One Sunday night when I was six, I contracted an ear infection that sent my temperature soaring to 104. In my feverish delirium, I believed I had swallowed an atomic bomb. I sat in the middle of my bed screaming, "Don't touch me or I'll blow up the world." Kids and dogs in our neighborhood surrounded my house and waited for the explosion. The doctor came and immersed me in a tub of cold water to lower my fever. I didn't explode.

No matter how funny this story is in hindsight, I still recall my utter terror. I read recently that one of the most overwhelming terrors of children is that one push of a button will end our world.

Growing Up in the Nuclear Age

Sometimes
I just sit
waiting for the tears to come
not understanding why.
Sometimes
the pit of my stomach
hurts for woods and fields and wind and lightning.
Sometimes
I think about the firefly jar I live in
afraid only
that someone will break the frail glass unintentionally
and I will lie helpless on the floor among the shards

wriggling my feet at the sky,
feeling the bulk of useless wings pinned beneath me.

—Stephanie Johnston

In this poem the speaker "hurts for woods and fields and wind and lightning." Her fear is not just for herself, but for the land, animals, and weather of planet earth. She ends her poem with an extended metaphor comparing her world to a "firefly jar," and its painfully fragile existence.

Here is another poem about the frailty of all life on earth:

Ground Zero

When I was young
we had a snake skin
pinned on our living room wall
beside the Japanese prints
and I used to wonder
about the snake who slithered
around raw
his skin in our possession

My Dad told me one day
that all snakes shed their skin once a year,
growing beneath a new skin
I never understood how they
knew when to shed it

One year I was hiking
and I saw a snake rubbing
up against a tree
the snake emerged as if
it was born from its old skin
shed upon the bark,
its new skin fresh
and glimmering in the sun
I almost picked the skin up to take
with me—but left it for the trees to
shed their leaves upon

Now, when the earth is well-worn
I wonder how we will know
when to pin ourselves upon the wall
in hopes that growing beneath
will be new skins to shed

—Tamarie Spielman

If the precarious balance of our planet's ecosystem were severely disrupted—by overpopulation, by the bomb, or by the greenhouse effect—what would you mourn the loss of? What images can you create to suggest your own fragility? Write.

SPACESHIP EARTH

It has been said that planet earth is like a spacecraft. What would happen on a spaceship if the water and oxygen ran out? Would you let a spaceship get overpopulated? In Tamarie's poem, "Ground Zero," what does this stanza ask?

> Now, when the earth is well-worn
> I wonder how we will know
> when to pin ourselves upon the wall
> in hopes that growing beneath
> will be new skins to shed

Many Native Americans believe that the earth actually feels pain. One old chief said, "Everywhere the white man touches the earth she is sore." Fast-write quickly, brainstorming images of the earth as a fragile cell or living being.

BOMB

Several years ago while attending school in England, I met a teacher from a third-world country. He told me that it was not uncommon for bombs to explode during school hours and that often automatic weapons could be heard nearby. That conversation convinced me of how thankful I should be for teaching in the United States. That same year I saw a simple and powerful painting called *Third World Primer*. (A primer is a reading textbook with pictures and verses.) On the painting the words *Womb*, *Bomb*, and *Tomb* were written. Under the first word was a triangle; under the second, a missile; and under *Tomb*, a wooden box. When I saw the art, I remembered the teacher's story. I sat down to imagine what primer I would use to teach in a war-torn world. My poem uses irony and exaggeration to make its point. Read it aloud.

Third World Primer

Children, say these words clearly:

WOMB   BOMB   TOMB

Place the palm of your hand to your lips,
close your eyes and say WOOOMB,
blowing the warm moist air between your fingers.
Now, using both hands, put your thumbs
together, then your forefingers. Form
a triangle over your navel, feel the shape
try to pull you back inside.

Now, say BOMB   BOMB   BOMB   BOMB

There can never be just one.
Ready? Quickly crawl under your work tables,
Kneel on your knees and place your head
to the floor. Cover your head with your hands
and begin to scream until everyone is screaming.
This means you're still alive.

Now without getting up, roll over on your back
and when the light is out, close your eyes
and imagine you feel the wooden table
close around you. Place the tip of your tongue
to the roof of your mouth, breath deeply and very
slowly say   TOOOMB.

—B. B.

Pretend you are the teacher of a class of these children. What would you tell them? Feel free to use grotesque images or irony. If you want to be ironic, let the tone of the voice be soft and the images brutal, building a tension between what is said and how it is said.

After this fast-writing, you might adopt the voice of one of the children. Tell about your daily routine. Are you afraid for your little sister, your parents? How important is learning the parts of speech when your home might become a pile of ashes?

GOOD ADVICE

"Go in fear of abstractions." So said the great poet and mentor of poets, Ezra Pound, and his advice is an important lesson for any writer.

Abstractions are names of concepts and emotions, like *justice* or *loneliness*. Such words may make your writing obvious, rather than subtle and indirect. The best poets heed Pound's caution; and instead of naming or explaining feelings and ideas, they recreate experience through concrete sensory detail and leave readers to respond with their own thoughts and emotions.

A good poem occasionally has an abstraction in it, but usually the poet has used enough concrete imagery to clarify the term and show more precisely what he means by the abstraction. Details earn a writer the right to use an abstraction every once in a while, and the reader isn't insulted by having the writer tell or explain a little.

1. Turn ahead to chapter 7 and read Sue Standing's "How To Be Angry" to someone. Don't read the title, just begin with the first line, "Instructions for the hour . . . " Have your listener name the emotion the poem is about. The imagery and figurative comparisons have made it so clear what emotion is being suggested that the title isn't necessary for an understanding of the poem.

2. Go through a draft and circle the abstractions. Revise by deleting all of them, allowing the details to suggest the feelings or ideas. If you find none to cut, Pound would be proud of you.

3. Now read one of your revised drafts to a friend, or several, and ask them to tell you the mood they feel, what they think. They will probably name an emotion very close to the one you had in mind. If the responses seem vague or wrong, don't be too quick to blame your readers. Try revising the draft by clarifying and sharpening the images, adding more details to make the experience more vivid. Then try the poem on some other readers.

INSTRUCTIONS FOR LIFE ON EARTH

Human beings would rather give advice or instructions than take them. It is no surprise to find that many poems advise and instruct; they come in a variety of voices, from funny to serious, sincere to ironic. Let's start with a playful one:

Instructions for a January Rainstorm

Choose a day with wind.
Wear unfashionable jeans and
a wool sweater in true colors.
Wear no shoes.
Look for an approachable tree.
It should have many branches and
much root wisdom.
Twist yourself up
through the vertical maze of twigs
until you are higher than

everything shaped by men.
Do not be afraid in the wind.
The tree has carried more
snow than your weight.
Find a branch that is strong,
that shapes to your body.
Hold the tree closely.
Wrap your legs around.
Trust it like a new friend
or old lover.
No one can see you now
except a red-tailed hawk
or misplaced seagull.
Sink close to sleep
in this dance
more graceful than a cradle rocking.
Even while the sky falls
in ribbons, you will be dry.
If you grow cold,
slip down with caution.
Make yourself hot ginger tea.
Watch the sky grow taller
toward the stars.
Do not remove the pine needles
from your hair
too soon.

—Jennifer Drake

Jennifer allows a reader to share the rich sensual texture of this
private experience. You can see "through the vertical maze of twigs,"
rock with "this dance / more graceful than a cradle" and smell the "hot
ginger tea."

Each of us has a storehouse of such experiences on which to draw.
Can you show someone how to wade a creek, listen to the wind in
trees, weave a sweater, throw a strike, or watch a sunset? Can you
teach how to avoid a little brother, how to act on a first date, how to
fail a test, throw a pot, or eat an ice cream cone? Give detailed instructions. Pay attention to the way the experience looks, smells, tastes,
and feels to the skin. Write.

In the next three poems, personae are speaking to specific individuals. In the first poem, an uncle is telling what he is afraid his niece

will lose by growing up. In the second, a father explains what his son will have to learn to be an adult, whether it is useful or not. The third is a teacher pleading with a student to stay awake and listen, to see if the play *Hamlet* might help them understand each other. Read them aloud as though you're speaking to the person addressed.

Advice to My Niece

When you age away from
the bashfulness of swing sets
and the lonely edge of school yards
to see yourself as a part
of useless conversations
with strangers waiting
at drinking fountains or
family meetings
filled with too much
talk and potato salad,
think about that little girl
who once considered a crowd
any number over two and
stood on the outside
observing the squirrel's eye
the freed pine needle
her own staunch separation from the group
and make a list of what
your loss of solitude
has allowed you to see.

—B. B.

To David, About His Education

The world is full of mostly invisible things,
And there is no way but putting the mind's eye,
Or its nose, in a book, to find them out,
Things like the square root of Everest
Or how many times Byron goes into Texas,
Or whether the law of the excluded middle
Applies west of the Rockies. For these
And the like reasons, you have to go to school
And study books and listen to what you are told,
And sometimes try to remember. Though I don't know
What you will do with the mean annual rainfall

On Plato's Republic, or the calorie content
Of the Diet of Worms, such things are said to be
Good for you, and you will have to learn them
In order to become one of the grown-ups
Who sees invisible things neither steadily nor whole,
But keeps gravely the grand confusion of the world
Under his hat, which is where it belongs,
And teaches small children to do this in their turn.

—Howard Nemerov

To Cathy, Sleeping in My Second Hour Class on *Hamlet*

Damn it, Cathy,
get your head up off the desk;
I'm not just reading words up here.
Hamlet's father's dead;
his mother and his uncle
have done some pretty rotten things to him.
His noble life's in danger.
His lover's dead: Laertes and Polonius
have shuffled off,
and Rosencrantz and Guildenstern
are pushing up the gilded roses
somewhere near Westminster hall.
The man is standing in a graveyard
staring at the chapless face of death.
Wake up and help him solve his problems;
it may perhaps do you some good.
Unfortunately, I can't say what.
I don't know all the twists and whirlwinds
of your passion.
We're separate. Can't we meet in Elsinor
and learn to understand
this Dane,
each other,
and ourselves?

—Richard Calisch

These poems are more like explanations than advice. I have the
feeling the narrators are speaking to themselves as well as to the
persons addressed. Whom would you advise if you could? Who could

learn from your mistakes? To whom do you feel you owe an explanation? Write as though you are speaking directly to the person: "Damn it, Cathy, / get your head up off the desk."

MORE ADVICE

The next two poems are narrated by parents. In "Lullabye for 17," a mother who is soon to lose her daughter to adulthood speaks to her about men. In the poem, "About Women," a father thinks about how foolish a man would be "to give his son the honest truth about women." His reaction to the woman on the beach and his description of his sleeping daughter suggest that the truth about women is not easily known.

Lullabye for 17

You are so young
you heal as you weep,
and your tears
instead of scalding
your face like mine
absolve
simply as rain.

I tried to teach you
what I knew: how men
in their sudden beauty
are more dangerous,
how love refracting light
can burn the hand, how memory
is a scorpion

and stings with its tail.
You knew my catechism
but never believed. Now
you look upon pain
as a discovery all your own,
marveling at the way it invades
the bloodstream, ambushes sleep.

Still you forgive
so easily, I'd like
to take your young man
by his curls and tear

them out,
who like a dark planet circles
your bright universe

still furnished with curtains
you embroidered yourself,
an underbrush
of books and scarves,
a door at which
you'll soon be poised
to leave.

—Linda Pastan

About Women

Who is more foolish than the poor man
who tries to give his son the honest truth
about women?
              When the boy is thirteen,
the man thinks back to how the world had to change,
how its giving curves began to fill him up,
and he wants to tell his son what it is
he has learned since then, what women
might mean in his life.

So he tells the boy Paul was surely wrong
when he said to the Corinthians
if a man could get by, not touching a woman,
that was good. He relates how Freud
died, still baffled by females. He pulls in
Darwin to explain why everyone turns
to watch a certain girl walk by.
                          And he talks
of Saturday mornings, when the sun slants in
through the bedroom window,
how his wife comes warm into his arms
to share the way the dust luxuriates in light,
to lie there and listen to the house as it settles,
to the rustling of children in the next room,
and to drift back, together.
                          But he thinks
of something he will keep to himself:
his desire for a woman at the beach last year.
She was old, slightly bent, not beautiful.

Her housedress trailed through the foam, gaped open
to the waist.
                    He is puzzled, uneasy,
remembering his daughter
in the mornings, how he finds her, tightly curled,
shivering, the quilt kicked off. How she wakes
facing any wall, turned at random, as if spun
like a bottle, unaware, though she has dreamed.

—Judson Mitcham

This assignment should be written from two perspectives:

1. Adopt one of your parent's voices. What would he or she say to you about members of the opposite sex?

2. From your own voice or a voice of someone your age, tell someone older than you what you know about the opposite sex. You might include what you wish you had known earlier, or what you could never have been prepared for.

7

Introspection

Our daily schedules get so hectic that we forget how complex the person is who stares back at us in the mirror when we brush our teeth. I hope by now the writing ideas in this book have taught you that your imagination and experience are rich with important stories, observations, and feelings—your best sources for subject matter.

The last two chapters have asked you to explore a world outside yourself. The writing ideas in this chapter will help you look inside, and they offer important possibilities for new poems. Before you fast-write on these ideas, get the folder that holds your drafts and poems. Thumb through it, reading the titles and skimming the poems. Think about the person who wrote them.

PAPER-BAG PEOPLE

Before you read this section, gather together these items: two grocery bags large enough to fit over your head, colored markers, crayons, sharp scissors, and a mirror. Have your own materials so no one will have to waste time borrowing.

In "A Paper Bag" by Margaret Atwood, the narrator makes a paper-bag mask the way she did when she was younger. She describes it and then addresses it directly.

A Paper Bag

I make my head, as I used to,
out of a paper bag,
pull it down to the collarbone,

draw eyes around my eyes,
with purple and green
spikes to show surprise,
a thumb-shaped nose,

a mouth around my mouth
penciled by touch, then colored in
flat red.

With this new head, the body now
stretched like a stocking and exhausted could
dance again; if I made a
tongue I could sing.

An old sheet and it's Halloween;
but why is it worse or more
frightening, this pinface
head of square hair and no chin?

Like an idiot, it has no past
and is always entering the future
through its slots of eyes, purblind
and groping with its thick smile,
a tentacle of perpetual joy.

Paper head, I prefer you
because of your emptiness;
from within you any
word could still be said.

With you I could have
more than one skin,
a blank interior, a repertoire
of untold stories,
a fresh beginning.

—Margaret Atwood

It was a cold winter day on the third story of an old building in the middle of a city. The sun hadn't shone in three weeks. The class was in a winter mood. The following pieces were written in that setting. In the first poem, the persona blends her self-doubts with the identity of the bag and can't remove it:

Grocery Bag Mask

I figured that I shouldn't start
with the side that said "Winn Dixie,"

but the one that was blank,
so I could look like I wanted to.
Magic Marker-blue eyes would be kind,
or I thought so anyway,

then I added a jungle
to make me a little bit hard to reach
from the outside. A safety feature.
And last, down where the mouth should be,
water, a babbling brook
so that I'm never sure what I'm saying.

There is no way that you and I
can both live here, bag.
People see your flat, ugly face
and think that's all there is,
that you're hollow,
but I'm inside and all I can
see is brown flecks, your insides,
and that's only when I have my eyes open.
Most of the time they're shut,
I pretend that you're not really there.

I want to rip you off
and tear you into a trillion pieces,
drop each one out the window
to be carried away by the wind,
swallowed by mud puddles.
But I am afraid,
that since I made you part of me,
I won't be different
once you're gone.

—Eleanor Womack

In Myra's draft she decided that no matter how she might change
her identity, she would certainly keep her color:

Creation of a New Me

Sometimes
everything in the world
is a reason
for a new me.
I pass people on the street
and they try hard

not to see the eyes
in my mask.
Wide eyes that sprinkle madness
whenever my cheek is turned.
If I could make a new mask
would there still be eyes
to see the roses
beside the sewer
or the rainbow
after the storm?
If I could make a new mask
there would be no eyes
to see the mother
who whispers in her baby's ear
say KKK say KKK,
but I would hear her mask cracking
into a smile.
If I could make a new mask
would there still be ears
to hear the black ball clicking
in every marble bag?
If I could make a new mask
there would be no ears
to hear your heart debate
whether or not to turn
my mask around
and see good
or bad but not
just brown.
If I could make a new mask
would the paper bag still be brown,
Yes,
that is all of the old one
that would be left.

—Myra K. Rucker

In the third poem the bag becomes a place to imprison dreams, like a bag used to drown puppies, and finally a shield to stop new possibilities from getting in, "like birds who fly against glass":

Untitled

Find me burying dreams in a paper sack
stuffing them in until it bulges wide as if

someone blew a lungful of air inside, bunched the open end
tight and slapped it hard with one palm.
Find me tying stones to the necks of memories
and dropping them from bridges, listen to the wail
like wet-warm puppies as the air screams around them.
Find me cleaning windows not so that visions won't escape,
more likely that they die trying to get in,
like birds who fly against the glass without ever seeing.

—Barry Gilmore

The fourth poem is very unusual because the narrator watches the
class make their bag masks. As she watches, she considers the masks
we all wear, "the many different faces we show from hour to hour":

Untitled

I watch you all in the mirror
your shapes fuzzy in the tarnished silver,
smiles dusty in the winter sunlight
that streams through the windows and over your backs.
Each of you has markers in hand,
laugh at the silly green and red faces
you have made.
One guy puts the bag over his head,
his nose protruding through the brown
paper skin. He dances a jig
around the yellow chair
and then plops down, cross-legged
takes off the mask and is himself again—
stiff and formal, a deep blush moving down his face
as laughter washes over him.
I could talk now about the masks
we all wear, about the bag that boy keeps
over his head, the many different faces
we show from hour to hour.
But as I watch your forms
flickering in reflection,
bags in hand,
I think it goes unsaid.

—Michele Gay

Make your mask any way you wish. It can be a face that reflects
your mood, a collage of many roles you play, or a mask revealing

what you would like to be. Make several—the clown, the child, the serious adult, or a face of a self you rarely show anyone. Work on this mask as long as you like. When you are finished, get off by yourself if possible. Try it on, look in a mirror, then take it off and set it in front of you as you write. Before beginning, reread the last two stanzas of Margaret Atwood's poem.

THEM BONES

Without my paper-bag mask, I am myself again. If I stand sideways before a full-length mirror, I notice the same head, shoulders, and waistline. My hands, arms, legs, and feet are still connected. Like it or not, this is me. Despite what some magazine and television commercials might suggest, no one is physically perfect. Even nicknames often reflect outstanding features: Slim Pickens, Red Warren, Minnesota Fats. Most of us dislike or are embarrassed about some flaw in our bodies. In the next poem the speaker tells about her legs.

Poem in Which My Legs Are Accepted

Legs!
How we have suffered each other,
never meeting the standards of magazines
                              or official measurements.

I have hung you from trapezes,
            sat you on wooden rollers,
            pulled and pushed you
                              with the anxiety of taffy,
and still you are yourselves!

Most obvious imperfection, blight on my fantasy life,
strong,
plump,
never to be skinny
or even hinting of the svelte beauties in history books
                              or Sears catalogues.

Here you are—solid, fleshy and
white as when I first noticed you, sitting on the toilet,
                              spread softly over the
                              wooden seat,

having been with me only twelve years,
                                              yet
as obvious as the legs of my thirty-year-old gym teacher.

Legs!
O that was the year we did acrobatics in the annual gym
     show.
How you split for me!

                    One-handed cartwheels
                    from this end of the gymnasium to
                         the other,
                         ending in double splits,
legs you flashed in blue rayon slacks my mother bought
     for the occasion
and tho you were confidently swinging along,
the rest of me blushed at the sound of clapping.

Legs!
How I have worried about you, not able to hide you,
embarrassed at beaches, in highschool
                    when the cheerleaders' slim brown legs
                              spread all over
                              the sand
                              with the perfection
                              of bamboo.
I hated you, and still you have never given out on me.

With you
I have risen to the top of blue waves,
with you
I have carried food home as a loving gift
                              when my arms began un-
                              jelling like madrilenne.

Legs, you are a pillow,
white and plentiful with feathers for his wild head.
You are the endless scenery
behind the tense sinewy elegance of his two dark legs.
You welcome him joyfully
and dance.
And you will be the locks in a new canal between
     continents.
                    The ship of life will push out of you
                    and rejoice

in the whiteness,
in the first floating and rising of

water.

—Kathleen Fraser

What started as a poem critical of her legs, ends with her accep-
tance and praise of them. These strong limbs will be the locks from
which new life will be born. This is a humorous, sensitive handling of
a delicate subject. Write a poem accepting your body or some part, or
parts, of it. Be specific. Deal with legs, feet, eyes, hands, nose, ears,
shoulders, or hair, for example.

THE REJECTION LETTER

The following poem, by Lyn Lifshin, plays on the impersonal,
pompous, and casually cruel rejection letter to a job applicant. She
jams together sentence fragments and ideas for ironic effect. Read it
silently first, then aloud.

You Understand the Requirements

We are
sorry to have to
regret to
tell you
sorry sorry
regret sorry that you have
failed

your hair should have been
piled up higher

you have failed to
pass failed
your sorry
regret your
final hair comprehensive
exam satisfactorily
you understand the requirements

you understand we are
sorry final

and didn't look as professional
as desirable
or sorry dignified
and have little enough
sympathy for 16th century
sorry english anglicanism
we don't know doctoral
competency what to think and
regret you will sorry not
be able to stay
or finish

final regret your disappointment
the unsuccessfully completed best
wishes for the future
it has been a
regret sorry the requirements
the university policy
please don't call us.

—Lyn Lifshin

Have you ever felt rejected by an institution, person, or group? Take on the voice of the rejecter and write a letter explaining why you're not good enough to succeed or to be included as a member.

FINDING YOURSELF AGAIN

"I am alone with the beating of my heart—"

—Lui Chi

Sometimes we feel most alone in a crowd. Solitude is neither negative nor positive. Often, we want to be by ourselves. The next poem is about being in a personal solitude seemingly outside of time:

Moving

Bookshelves empty, tables lampless; walls
bare, the house is a rubble of moving—
foothills of boxes, trunks
under clouds of ceiling.

                              My friends
said good-bye hours ago, when June twilight
hung on the hills. Now, in late dark
muggy for stars, moths whir at the yellow porch light,
ping screens. By the one dim floor lamp
among the shadowy undoings of my life,
in a limbo between having gone and having gone,
I sit like a caretaker of my doom.
Not an ashtray or a spoon.
In the real dawn, I will be going.

My friends are sleeping, turned toward
tomorrows without me—will still be sleeping
when I begin to drive the familiar streets and roads
in which sun will come only after me.
If I called them now, in this hollow
past midnight, anything I said would
be from the future.

                    Alone in the present,
I wait, smoking (a tin can for ashes).
Bugs thwack on the screens. Beyond love
I am a projectile into the future—
still hours, days away.
Time has stopped at the speed I am going, landmarks
appear strangely in new light,
clouds whirling past me, into the past.

The phone has been disconnected.

                                        —Robert Wallace

In "Moving" all personal possessions are packed, good-byes have been said, and the phone has been disconnected. The speaker is trapped in "this hollow past midnight" with a lonely present. The future is "still hours, days away."

Visualize your home. Picture it empty of all your belongings. Everyone you know thinks you have already gone. Fast-write the experience in first person.

TEACHING EMOTIONS

How To Be Angry

Instructions for this hour: First, breathe
as shallowly as you can. Pretend you hear

the sound of a door slamming over and over,
its bright clang, then muffled reverberation.
Your heart beats more quickly until your hands
make involuntary fists that knock against each other,
like the hearts of strangers. Second, pretend
you are a diamondback rattler. Narrow your eyes.
Be one long sinew of focused malice, your glance
a wedge of muscle pressed against your enemy.
Then, think of cold air whirring through cracks,
dinosaur eggs unhatched in Montana buttes,
the anteater's tongue, the bullet holes
in a target, the lies in your enemy's mouth.

—Sue Standing

Pick an emotion you would really like to express, one that you could teach someone else to feel: love, sorrow, joy, pity, numbness, fear, strength, weakness. Following the example of the poem, "How To Be Angry," instruct a class how to express that emotion. Before you write, though, go back to chapter 6 and read the section "Good Advice."

"MIRROR, MIRROR ON THE WALL"

We need no more than a few minutes spent studying magazines and TV ads to realize how much we value white teeth, slim figures, sparkling hair, and stylish clothes as symbols of personal success. It's no wonder that we are encouraged to look at ourselves in the mirror several times a day. But if mirrors could talk, what would they say about our poking our mugs in their faces? In this poem, Sylvia Plath gives the mirror a voice:

Mirror

I am silver and exact. I have no preconceptions.
Whatever I see I swallow immediately
Just as it is, unmisted by love or dislike.
I am not cruel, only truthful—
The eye of a little god, four-cornered.
Most of the time I meditate on the opposite wall.
It is pink, with speckles. I have looked at it so long
I think it is a part of my heart. But it flickers.
Faces and darkness separate us over and over.

Now I am a lake. A woman bends over me,
Searching my reaches for what she really is.
Then she turns to those liars, the candles or the moon.
I see her back, and reflect it faithfully.
She rewards me with tears and an agitation of hands.
I am important to her. She comes and goes.
Each morning it is her face that replaces the darkness.
In me she has drowned a young girl, and in me an old woman
Rises toward her day after day, like a terrible fish.

—Sylvia Plath

In this poem, a mirror has witnessed a young girl change into an older woman. If the mirrors in your house could talk, what would they tell of the people who peer into them? Think about your daily routines, then choose a mirror and have it speak.

THE PERSON YOU ARE LOOKING AT

At the beginning of this chapter, I suggested that you thumb through your writing folder to look back over the drafts and poems you have written. Please do that again now.

Some of your work is based on real events, some may be pure fiction, and most are probably a combination. Memory is how we think things used to be. All of your drafts are important products of your imagination. Now read the following poem:

The Man You Are Looking At

is someone you ought to know.
You were always together.
But seeing him speak
of stocks and bonds
and weather patterns
you kid yourself
how happy you are
for his success,

when in fact you daydream
about a boy who believed
he could leave his body
and walk beneath evening sycamores
to sing for the trees.

The boy who promised you
beyond your heartbeats
until your breath swung back,
inhaling the eternity of death,
that you would be for each
one heartbeat to the end.

But seeing him here, you feel
only the chill of wanting
to startle him with the promise
he made you long ago. Instead,
you splash cold water in your face
and straighten your tie—
you can't be late for the office.

—Robert E. Haynes

Close your eyes and picture yourself at a mirror. Address that
person you see, the one you ought to know.

8

Voices Within,
Voices Without

In public places it's hard to avoid hearing bits of other people's conversations:

> He's cute, but his breath could exterminate flies.
> I can't even afford to eat at no White Tower no more.
> You've got spinach on your teeth, dear.

Out of a natural curiosity, we observe other people's actions and talk. Conversation, combined with setting and situation, is excellent subject matter for poetry. Speech, posture, and mannerisms reveal important details of everyday life. The following poems include overheard conversations and observed actions. They are brief accounts that present character, setting, and situation with an economy and compression not usually possible in prose.

Landscape, 1986

You're in a fast food place
and this plain old guy
sits down at the table across from you.

He's got on two year old Knapp boots,
soiled in the way work soils, and his coat
is like one you'd see on a 4th grader
in Buffalo, orange and green and yellow
checks, a fake sheepskin collar,

polyfill guts spilling out down by the kidney.
It's dinnertime and before him
is a cardboard dish with 99 cent fries
and a cardboard cup of coffee hot enough
to scald. The mouth

in his day old beard
starts moving, even though he's alone,
and you know he's speaking,
not to you as you eye your food,
but to God. To God. This happened

last night
and all you can think of
today is some sad kid in Buffalo
learning the prayers he'll need to grow up
in America.

—Paul McRay

Two at the Library

While this tiny frail wild-eyed
Old lady dressed in blue
Keeps saying, "No go" as she
Checks her lottery tickets in the
Paper, a bearded old man sitting
Across the table from her
Cleans his nails with a pocket knife
And looks at a movie star album.
His eyes are tiny slits.
"I hate this town," she says.
"You hear me, Bob? No one cares.
No one gives a damn."
"Yeah," he replies. "Inflation's
So bad," she says, "I can't even
Afford to eat at no White Tower
No more. Are you dead, Bob?"
He pulls his hat brim down over his eyes.
"This is a helluva place to be, Bob."

—Gary Pacernick

In the All-Night Laundromat

I wash my sheets at dawn.
The air is muggy, milky white.

Across the street, a thin man
sways out of Jay's All-Night Jazz Garden
with a plastic cup in his hand.
He tipped me a ten two hours ago.
Now, he does a little two step
on the curb, gracefully bows
to no one, and walks away.

A woman comes in through the place
where a door belongs.
Her dark face is stitched in
like a nylon stocking doll.
A brown baby rests on her hip,
garbage bags in her other arm.
She looks at me,
at the wooden benches,
then at the huge broken window
where a Pontiac ended up last week.
We are alone in the world
of soap and water.

I warn her, that first machine is busted,
takes your change, but then won't spin.
"Honey," she says, "I know
all about it," pointing with her hip,
baby and all, and whispers,
"Don't feed *that one* a dime,
this one here works for nothin."

—Ellen M. Taylor

Winn-Dixie at Closing on a Winter Tuesday Night

Automatic doors push open,
the cold winter air flooding in
as I bend over my register.
It is dark out, late—I am cleaning
the scanner and it is clicking softly.
The box of Winstons is thrown at my fingers,
"Do ya have ta be 18 to buy these here?"
His voice is daring me, I look into
his eyes—older than 18 in a young man's face.
His hair is long and unruly, a slight
brown fuzz grows over his lips—mouth set
in calm indignation.

I nod yes, trying hard not to blush.
My hands clench the wiping cloth
(I could have told him he could buy them—
no one would have known if he hadn't asked)
and I am not deaf to his eyes' message
even as he turns to stalk out
through the automatic doors.

—Tracy Cotton

Listen for bits of talk that surprise you. Then get them down, see where they lead. To get a start, close your eyes and see a public place— a mall, church, synagogue, bus stop, park, fast-food joint, any place. Fast-write an overheard conversation and see where it takes you.

During the next week, carry a pen and note pad to jot down important details of setting, gesture, and conversation. If this moves you into a fast-writing on the spot, do it. Don't worry about who is around. (Maybe they'll write about you.) Remember, the poem doesn't have to make a statement, and it may not end quite the way you expected. Maybe it will surprise you. Often that's the way the best poems happen to their writers.

Bring your observations to class to share with classmates. Bounce off each other's notes into new writings. Try several points of view:

1. As in "Landscape 1986," let an observation of a person's dress and behavior start you into a writing. Try it in second person, "you": "You're in a fast food place."

2. Take down snatches of an overheard conversation. Arrange it so that your writing captures characters in a dramatic moment, like "Two at the Library." Try this one in third person. Give the reader brief, but telling, details and actions, such as cleaning fingernails with a pocket knife.

3. Try one in first person, "I," like "In the All-Night Laundromat." Include details of setting and use direct quotations.

VOICES FROM LITERATURE

In the summer of my tenth year, Tommy Hoover was Huck Finn and I was Tom Sawyer. We would carry hobo sacks tied on sticks and, sneaking from oak to hedge, pretend we were being followed. When we got to the fallen elm, Huck and I grabbed our limbs from under the trunk, and in our imaginations, poled our way across a Mississippi

River cove to a secret island. We had been captivated by the power of fiction, and Mark Twain's characters lived on in our summer adventures. We helped slaves escape, pulled dead bodies from the river, and got lost in a cave full of treasure.

In the next poem a student chose the voice of a character in a current novel, *One Day of Life* by Manuel Artuega. The speaker reveals the harsh economic and political conditions of the character's country.

My José
(*in the voice of Guadalupe Fuentes*)

My José,
What can be said about this morning
when the men in their brown and green uniforms
dragged you, half dead, to my doorstep.
The blood on your face seemed to fall
towards the dusty ground as if your blood
was no more than dew, falling from a chilamantes tree.

The men that brought you were clean,
proper and unsmiling. Somehow their faces
set in hard expression
seemed carved out of stone.

What could I say,
when they asked if I knew you?
I, your wife,
sat on our dusty porch
and knew,
when you looked up at me with the one eye
now beaten shut,
what I should do.

The clarinero bird cried, José,
and I stared at the uniformed men
like a child stares at a man
who has lost a limb.

I told them I did not know you,
so your children play safely
in the small brook behind our house.

The sky, José, will be red with your blood tonight.
It will cry out for you this one evening
and your children will know you are gone.

—Vanessa Cain

In "To Atticus" Becky Bice speaks for the character Scout in Harper Lee's novel:

To Atticus
—From *To Kill A Mockingbird*

Atticus Finch,
I listened to you
(for once)
and walked around
in ol' Boo's skin.
I think I understand
what you were talkin' about.
At first,
I got pretty upset
when I heard
you was gonna
represent Tom
at the trial.
I know now
why you accepted
those turnip greens
for payment,
and how the Negroes paid
you back for defendin' Tom,
by sendin' hunks of salt ham,
beans, and scuppernongs.

And Atticus,
I s'pose Jem and I
well, we'll grow up
somehow—and
I'll never shoot a mockingbird.
Those flowers in Ms. Dubose's yard
are growin' back
and Aunt Alexandria
has got me in this dumb dress.
I don't see nothin' proper
'bout it!

Let me sit in your lap
one more time.
Me, Miss Jean Louise Finch.

Maybe you'll read
some of the paper to me.
Now—
I can call you Father.

—Rebecca Bice

Max Otterland begins his poem as the observer of a scene that takes place in George Orwell's novel *1984*. And then Max allows the two main characters of the book to speak, each telling his or her perceptions of the one moment of freedom and joy they share.

1984

1984: The washer woman washes
and sings songs
written by machines
making them beautiful
as she hangs up the laundry
which isn't really clean.

Winston and Julia watch her
from the nook
with the windowsill
drinking coffee
synthesized by computers
which tastes real
though from no roasted bean.

For now
there is no Elvis
and there is no Columbia,
there are just two bodies

naked and imperfect
turning into dust, naturally.

Winston: Daydreaming to the first time . . .
I looked through the cafe window,
"there under the chestnut tree
I saw her and she saw me"

At the moment
I see her
waiting in the bed
naked and imperfect.

The items which she brought
lying beside her,
real coffee, tea, chocolate.

Slipping beneath the sheets
I dream of the way things were
when men and women
ran through fields
and fed each other real fruit.

Julia: Yes, he is asleep now
and the sun is setting fast.
I see his face
as it would be at death
so pallid and empty.
He is wrinkled—old looking
yet no older than I

In this day
we begin life
with the orange of dusk
already much advanced.

It does not matter
as long as my job is accomplished.
Come now thought-police
take this old finished man
take him for worthless.

                                    —Max Otterland

Choose a character from a work of literature that excites you and
have that character comment on an event in his or her life. Have the
narrator speak to a close relation, as in "My José" or "To Atticus."
Insure the authenticity of the voice by including details of setting, like
"the small brook behind our house" or "the nook / with the windowsill." Try making comparisons, such as "I stared at the uniformed
men / like a child stares at a man / who has lost a limb."

VOICES FROM FAIRY TALES

The poem "Aschenputtel" by Peter Stillman is a retelling of the old
fairy tale all of us heard when we were children. Get in a story-telling
mood and read this aloud. Try to capture the tone of voice.

Aschenputtel

You couldn't blame her for losing her
composure, forgetting to take off
the other shoe, what with chocolate-
colored bats whiffling past her face and
not two minutes out from under all
those blazing chandeliers. A mad day,
and just the perfect ending: hobbling
pell-mell down an unlit road trailing
caveats and pumpkin rind.

What a showy, vaudeville stunt. All that
hocus-pocus with the tinny wand,
and the gown did absolutely nothing for
her eyes and the brocade scratched like
chickenwire, and you try dancing on a
marble floor in glass shoes without breaking
your neck. But the lowest—her bookish
father would have said "most egregious"—
trick of all was changing that goodlooking
coachman back into a rat.

What, after all, was she rushing for?
There are no muggers in a fairytale,
the woods are safe enough. She'd gone
out wandering at midnight once, when
the moon was big enough so you
could see a stump for what it was,
and moths the color of a wedding dress
had come sleepily up from the grass.
Her sisters would cavort like Percherons
'til dawn, then snore away the day,
their dank, clay-smelling gowns left dumped
for her to gather up.

A fox crossed the road on some unmagical
business. She stopped, pulled off
the other shoe, and flung it high enough
to wink like a firefly. They hadn't fit
in the first place, and why keep just
the one, even for a souvenir.

—Peter Stillman

Choose a fairy tale or nursery rhyme that you know well and rewrite it. You might want to review the original for plot and detail. But feel free, as you narrate the story, to alter the setting, plot, details, or tone. Have fun with this. Just think what you can do with the three little pigs in New York City, or a version of "Little Red Riding Hood" that doesn't end happily ever after, or a Goldilocks who chases off the three bears.

What happens to minor characters in fairy tales? Have you ever wondered how they felt? In "Subplot," we hear from Cinderella's coachman:

Subplot

Accident or the gods,
Processes busy about their own directions
Touch you, transform you. I found myself
Six feet tall,
Dressed in coachman's piping, a whip coiled
In my right hand—and in my stomach
The same half-digested cricket.
Oh, I remembered—the rat still crouched
In my brand-new brain, and I could almost
Twitch my nonexistent whiskers.
Far below, I saw the bricks of the floor
Ripple for miles. Out of the window,
I saw, for the first time, hills,
Truncated with evening light. Later
When I drove up the road,
There would be brightnesses overhead
I thought of as stars.

It became dark. She bent over once
To put on her shoes, hand against the mantel,
Each breast succulent, dependent
Against her bodice, the fire
Flickering on their curves. Her hair fell over
Her shoulders like water.

Sitting in the coach outside the dance,
I had hours to settle it all.
Laughter rang from the lighted windows,
Music drifted out. The horses
Whuffled and shuddered. Water lapped

On the stones of the palace pool.
Leaves whispered. Mosquitoes whined and bit me.
I couldn't bring myself to kill them.
I had hours to settle it all.
If I had touched her or run away,
They would have changed me back.
I had hours, hours,

Then the doors burst open, flooding the yard
With light and clamor,
And she fled down the steps like a bird.
All the way back down that country road,
The silver, impassive moon
Rode in the sky in front of me. I lashed blood
From those foaming backs,
I shouted scripture and algebra,
"I will turn blank eyes to the moon," I cried,
"The rest of my nights! I will be clubbed to death
Gnawing on a dead child's foot!"

—Jack Butler

Brainstorm a list of these bit players—like the mirror in "Snow White," Little Red Riding Hood's grandmother, or Rapunzel's hairdresser. You can probably think of even better ones; make your list, then choose one, and let he, she, or it have a say.

VOICES FROM HISTORY

In the following poem, the speaker imagines what would have happened if a Nazi concentration camp had never existed. In taking this approach, the poet impresses on the reader what atrocities did take place.

Revising History

Wake up, friends,
there's been a hoax—
you never died
at Auschwitz.

Come, relax,
soak your feet;
pick your teeth,
the gold-filled ones.

What makes stripes
on your coat?
A rising moon,
bands of light.

Yellow star
upon your chest?
It fell to earth,
heaven's gift.

And the smell
of burning flesh?
A dybbuk hides
in chimney smoke.

All is well,
rest in peace;
you never died
at Auschwitz.

—Gertrude Rubin

Choose an historical event: the Kennedy assassination, the invention of the airplane, the discovery of penicillin, the creation of the atomic bomb, the Viet Nam War. Rewrite history. What happened instead? What can you reveal about the importance of an event by having it never occur?

THE ELEMENTS OF VOICE

Poems must be heard as well as seen. You can learn quite a lot about a poem, yours or someone else's, by reading the poem aloud and listening for the elements of sound and music in the words.

Have someone read you a draft they've written. Try not to listen for content and meaning, but to the sounds—the flow of words, the way consonants bounce off each other, the way vowels contrast with or echo each other. Listen for the music—the harsh and punchy sounds, the liquid and soothing ones. Listen for the flow and pace of the words—the way the poem moves along with pressing insistence or lolls along lazily.

Have your partner go into the next room and read to you from about fifteen feet away, through a half-open door. That will help you concentrate on sound, rather than meaning. You may notice that the sounds suggest the tone and mood of the poem—whether it is solemn or bouncy and humorous, angry or lazy and mellow.

FINDING YOUR OWN VOICES

In this book we have implied that a writer needs to find his or her own voice, yet in this chapter we have asked you to try on various voices that aren't your own. The truth is that every writer can extend him- or herself to include other voices. It isn't difficult if you explore voices familiar to you. In a sense, the personae or voices of characters may actually be aspects or facets of your own voice.

A novelist or dramatist learns to allow characters to speak for themselves, and poets and prose writers do the same. The process is like role playing or playing a character on stage. The novelist Charles Dickens would get into character in front of a mirror and act out scenes before writing them down. Many other writers do the same thing, in their imaginations. It may be that trying on some of the voices you hear around you (or in your own head) may actually help you discover and shape your own unique voice.

In this chapter we suggest ways you might read aloud the poems we have given as examples. You should practice reading your own poems and drafts aloud, too. A big part of finding your own voice is simply paying attention to it, listening for it.

Reading a poem aloud is an art in itself. If you're reading a poem or a draft you've written, read your words as if they were written as prose, with this one exception: pause *slightly*—something like half a comma—at the end of each line to give the listener a subtle sense of the lineation. The following exercises in reading aloud will help you:

1. Read one of your drafts from the first part of this chapter into a tape recorder. Get into character and act out your poem, over-doing it if you want to. When you listen back, you may decide that the parts where you overacted don't really sound like you. Record the poem again, this time toning it down, making it feel more natural to you as you read. Listen again.

    Recording and rerecording your reading is like revising drafts; you can learn a great deal from the changes you make.

2. Turn on the tape recording of your poem and then go into the next room or far enough away that you hear only sounds but not distinct words. Listen to the music of your voice as it rises and falls, as it emphasizes or blurs syllables. Word music is a vital element of poetry, and this is one way of tuning into it.

3. Get together with one or two other writers. Swap drafts and read aloud to your group; help each other make the readings more effective. Look for places the reader might pause or slow down, emphasize or speed up, places the pitch or volume might be changed for a clearer or more effective reading.

4. It is very helpful to hear your writing voice coming across to you in the speaking voice of someone else, especially if the poem is a dramatic monologue or uses voices of characters. Hearing your words expressed through the mind and voice of someone else may help you notice things you want to change.

9

Stories Within—
And Beyond

Three years ago I was backpacking in the Cumberland Mountains with students. Exhausted by a hard day's trek, we slung our packs down beside a crystal stream. A worn park sign read, "Charit Creek." The brook could be heard rushing through the canyon like wind in a grove of hemlock. Around the blaze of a midnight campfire, we imagined how the creek got its name. One person said that *Charit* was the mountain pronounciation of *chariot,* and that the water rushed down the mountain like a chariot. Another said that the brook trout that inhabited the stream were char, and the stream's name was related to the fish. The question wasn't settled; we doused the fire and crawled into our sleeping bags for the night.

In the morning an old man told us that once the most beautiful girl in Station Hollow was named Charity and that she had fallen into the swollen creek one winter and drowned. He said that his mother had told him this story and that it had happened a hundred years ago. He drew us a map to her tombstone. That day I sat on a large rock beside the creek and conjured Charity's story.

Charit Creek

Charity, you had crossed the wide beech log
a hundred times to visit Station Hollow.
When you didn't return by late afternoon
your father took cedar knots from the shed,
lit a lantern and traced the path
to Branch Creek crossing.

In an eddy a hundred yards down
he witnessed the light flicker on your
long brown hair as it swirled
in the current like river kelp.
You hung U-shaped, caught at the waist
on a birch log; one white arm flapped
as if it meant to touch your toes.
He told Jake Hatfield that he couldn't
pull you out himself; the night held
the memory of your hazel eyes, the slight
blush of cheek, the thin lips which parted
when you smiled.
Over a hundred years later
an old man mentions this to me,
how he heard Charit Creek got its name.
I sit on a boulder to conjure your story
from the feel of this winter day.
High above, the buzzards circle the stone bluffs.
White sycamore bones reflect from the water.
They wind and flap as the wind shudders the surface.
These stark arms make the snow whiter,
and I think of you, dear Charity,
the awful look upon your face
as the limbs reach out against the gray sky
wearing starlings like clothes pins.

—B. B.

A legend is a story handed down from the past. It's important for us to preserve legends, to retell them so that they always seem new. Go legend hunting. Ask your parents, grandparents, or neighbors to tell you family or neighborhood stories. Is there a haunted house on your street? What's the story behind it? Legends can be as simple as how an uncle got a nickname, or as historical as the name of your street, town, or county. Look at a map of your area and find interesting names of streams, hills, mountains, buildings, or roads. Are there battle fields or archeological sights? Any of these could lead to an interesting story.

On a map of the area where I live, there are names like "Clay Lick Road," "Panther Creek," "Sinking Creek," "Buffalo River," "Fire Scald Knob," "Defeated Camp Run," and "Forked Deer River." Dig out a map of your own region. Whether you live in the city or the country, there is almost always a story behind naming. Here are some ways to approach writing about the material you find:

1. Preserve a family or neighborhood legend by presenting it in a poem. Write it in third person as in "Charit Creek."
2. Find an historical event that happened near your home—battle, early settlement, invention, anything. Become a character and re-live the event from an individual's point of view, in the first person.
3. Conjure a story explaining how a stream, mountain, building, park, marsh, swamp, island, or road got its name. If you don't know the story, create it from the name itself. (Example: "Fire Scald Knob" must have been the site of a terrible fire.) You might create a group of images that paints a picture of the place and shows how it got its name.

BECOMING A LEGEND IN YOUR OWN TIME

My Uncle Dan's name was Charles. I mean the name he was given at birth was Charles. He was called Dan because when he was a boy he thought he was Daniel Boone and spent all of his time playing at being a pioneer. My grandfather called him Dan and it stuck. I was twenty before I found out his real name.

The following two poems are translations by Howard Norman from the Swampy Cree Indian language. They tell the stories about how two people earned their names:

Quiet Until the Thaw

Her name tells of how
it was with her.

The truth is, she did not speak
in winter.
Everyone learned not to
ask her questions in winter,
once this was known about her.

The first winter this happened
we looked in her mouth to see
if something was frozen. Her tongue
maybe, or something else in there.

But after the thaw she spoke again
and told us it was fine for her that way.

So each spring we
looked forward to that.

> —from the Swampy Cree
> (translated by Howard Norman)

Got Dizzy

This name happened
under hawks.
When he was young he stood
facing UP, watching hawks
fly in circles.

Those hawks would hunt in circles
and you could see him turn too,
trying to keep up!

So, then, by doing this
he made a hawk begin circling
inside his head and feet.
BOTH PLACES IN HIM GOT DIZZY!

Sometimes
he fell.

In the morning
when a hawk flew out of a cloud
or tree to hunt, he was waiting.

—from the Swampy Cree
(translated by Howard Norman)

In the Cree language, names describe the personality, actions, or physical appearances of people. If I had been named after my younger years, I might have been called "small child who hates squash."

On a piece of scratch paper, brainstorm a list of words that describe your habits, actions, hobbies, likes, and dislikes. Then give yourself a nickname. Fast-write or draft the legend of how you got your name. If your piece turns out strange or mysterious, so be it. It belongs to you.

MORE WORDS FROM THE CREE

My students attended a workshop where Howard Norman showed a film and talked about the culture of the Swampy Cree Indians. Two of the Indian practices interested them more than other aspects of that rich culture. After the Cree have eaten meat, they hang the animal's bones in the trees by the river so that other creatures can't violate them. This is an act of reverence for the spirit of the animals that the Indians must eat to survive. The Cree Indians spare their children the horror of nightmares by having a special nightmare midwife take the bad dreams from the young. When we spent a week fast-writing about different aspects of the workshop, hanging bones and the nightmare midwife were written about most.

These two student poems are a result of that workshop:

The Dream Midwife

The dirt sifting through my fingers is dark
like the night pressing in around me.
I hear the wind rustling in the pines
and the steady sighs of his breath.
It will come soon,
when his eyes race beneath their lids
and the blankets jump on his chest.
I will wait quietly until then,
for the birth.
And when he cries the wolverine has come,
I will pull its shaggy fur, and hiss
at its gleaming teeth.
Fighting the claws that reach
for thoughts, not skin, I will close my eyes
and tug it slowly from his dreams.
Slinging it onto my back, I'll feel
it sink inside me, then slip silently
from the hobe back into moonlight.
The whistle of the night through bones
lashed to the trees and the sleeper's
slow breaths are enough to silence
the growls.

—Scholle Sawyer

The Nightmare Midwife

Outside
bleached bones crackle
in the wind,
hang restless from a wooden totem
as mama gathers bundles
of fir branches
to make the floor
we will sleep on tonight.

Father is gone again.
This time hunting
whatever winter will offer.
Gun in hand
he starts off through the trees,
the ice beneath his feet
losing its radiance with each step.

It is only now
that we need more food.
The nightmare midwife
has been here six days.
Tsai screams about a bear
who hovers over him each night,
saliva dripping from its mouth
onto the white fur blanket.
But the midwife stays,
choking on raw consonants
with every twitch
of Tsai's body.

It is she
who will birth his worst nightmare
screaming,
pushing him
into a new day,
the purple sun in her hair
as she hangs the silent bones
of the dream bear
softly on the totem.

                                    —Michele Gay

   Fast-write about a child having a nightmare taken from him. It can
be told in first or third person. The story can be narrated by the
dream-troubled child, a brother or sister, a parent, or the midwife
herself.

THE WORLDS OF SUPERSTITION

There are all sorts of ways of getting at the truth. Twisting the stem of
an apple and calling off the letters of the alphabet with each turn to
discover the initial of your true love may seem ridiculous in a literal

and factual sense, but a poem about ways of naming a spouse may give us a different sense of ourselves, and we may discover an emotional truth about the uncertainties we feel about so important a decision as choosing a mate. Often superstitions grow out of legends, and they are useful as cautionary tales. A young girl tending her small brother would do well to heed the superstition that says an infant's shadow should not cross an open well. Legends and superstitions make such advice easier to remember.

Many superstitions involving herbal cures, thought for many years to be silly, have been proven by science to be quite true. Milk *does* contain a chemical that induces sleep, and warming the milk makes the chemical work more quickly; so that old remedy for sleeplessness really does work.

Some superstitions have lost the legends that might explain them or give them some validity. Others, which grew out of misinformation or insecurity, are obviously not worth preserving, and we do well to see them for what they are—blindly held prejudices and practices based on ignorance or fear.

All human cultures have legends, superstitions, and mythologies to help explain the world. Myths involve whole systems of beliefs, rituals, and practices. Preserving such aspects of culture and civilization has been one of the missions of writers from the time of the bards many centuries ago.

Go back to the "Introduction to the Writer" and read the fast-writing by Vicki Chezem, in which she recounts an experience she had as a young girl—a very early (and very real) encounter with a superstition. You should be able to tell from the story what superstitious belief lies behind the experience. Now read the poem Vicki distilled from that fast-writing:

The Thresh-Healer

The old country folk call me Thresh-healer
    because my father died before I was born.
When I was five
    a lady named 'Lisbeth brought
      her sick baby
        to my aunt's house.
She sat in a big rocking chair with
    that baby draped across her lap
      just even with my face.
My brothers dragged me over to 'Lisbeth
    and that baby and everyone wanted to see

me breathe into that baby's mouth.
They were disappointed when I ran away
  to hide from them.
    My heart beat so loudly
      I knew they would find me
      hid behind that old wash-stand
  and they did.
Mam's shame was hard to bear
  and she was angry with me too.
    I must heal that baby
      or get a spanking
    so I crouched there, crying.
Uncle Daddy appeared over Mother's shoulder
  and asked to speak to me, alone.
He held me against his chest and I
  listened to the sound of his heart-beat.
He told me I didn't have to breathe
  into that baby's mouth if I didn't want to
    but it might help the baby if I did.
I didn't have to breathe into that baby's mouth
  if I didn't want to, but it would make him happy
    and he would carry me down to the corner store
    and buy me a box of Cracker Jacks if I would.
He carried me back to 'Lisbeth and her baby and
  made everyone leave but me and him.
We walked up to that baby together and
  I leaned over
    and breathed into its mouth.

—Vicki Chezem

What superstitions do you practice? Many people *practice* superstitions even though they don't *believe* in them. Do you still avoid
stepping on cracks in the sidewalk? I do. And I feel a little foolish
when I realize I'm unconsciously adjusting my stride to miss the
cracks—a silly habit I picked up back in first grade. I need to write a
poem about that.

Brainstorm a list of superstitions you practice, or know about.
Then pick one of them and do a fast-writing or a draft about it.

Foretelling

Folklore books list many superstitions that explain how people can find
the identity of their future spouses. The next poem reveals one way.

Mary Nell

The young girl with the No. 6 skillet hair
left the cabin with its noisy collage of children
to seek out old Widow Moresby who lived on top of the bluff
above Springhouse Creek.
She was known all through Jackson County
as the wise woman who'd told Uncle Dewey
where to find the lightning
his father'd hid from the excise men.
Mary had a different problem. She wanted to catch
young Carl with the azure Irish eyes.
That night and the next two she slept with a mirror
under her pillow.
On the third night she dreamed of Carl
and saw ten bright towheaded children:
Ina Belle, Helen Sue, Margaret, Joann, and Mary;
Charles, Gene, Roger, and the baby of the family, John L.,
and further another row, two of them twins,
and dimmer still the third, some simply round blurs.
Those she would never see.

—Wendolyn Bozarth

The girl with the No. 6 skillet hair slept with a mirror under her pillow and eventually was able to dream her future husband, children, and grandchilden. Wendy Bozarth wrote this poem using a superstition she read in a farmers' almanac. She made her grandmother the young girl in the poem because she was working on a group of poems about her family. Jackson County and Springhouse Creek are real places in Tennessee where her relatives live. Although Wendy used the names of real places and people, her poem is a blend of the real and down-to-earth with the fanciful and mysterious.

More Ideas

The following list of superstitions all explain how a person can identify his future marriage partner. Choose one and fast-write a story in which a character uses the superstition to see into the future. Using the names of real people and places might help to enrich and authenticate the poem.

1. Sleep with a mirror under your pillow and you will dream the face of your future spouse and children.

2. A young woman who eats a boiled egg whose yolk cavity is filled with salt will dream of being lost in the desert and the man who rescues her will be her future husband.

3. When you hear the first turtledove in the spring, turn around three times, then remove your shoe and stocking from the right foot. Look in the heel of the stocking, and you will find the color of your future husband's hair.

4. If you want to learn the first name of your future spouse, you can do so by sleeping in one of last season's cornfields on the first day of May. Wrap yourself in a clean white sheet, and during the night you will dream his or her face.

5. Make up one of your own and swear that some old gypsy read it to you from a crystal ball.

Yet More Possibilities

Here is a list of superstitions you can choose from for ideas for more poems:

1. Legend has it that when someone dies and is laid out at home, a member of the family must cover every mirror; for anyone who sees a reflected image of the deceased will die within a year.

2. Lay one tansy leaf on the navel to promote childbearing.

3. A mountain legend claims that when an infant smiles, he is consorting with angels.

4. To ensure that the firstborn son will have good luck and will avoid the curse of old Urim, all of the father's hats must be burned at the child's birth.

5. To find out your true enemy, mark ten-cent pieces with the initials of those people you suspect are your enemies. Then place the coins face (heads) down in a basin of cold water. Now bring the water to a boiling point. When you remove the basin from the fire, the coin turned face up will reveal your enemy.

6. A New England superstition claims that meeting a hunchback on the way to church will bring thirty days of bad luck; but the bad luck will be neutralized if one avoids church that day, or meets a second hunchback before entering the church.

7. You can stop a witch's spell by tossing a handful of dry apple seeds over your left shoulder with your right hand on a cloudless night when the moon is full.

8. Tossing rice on a newly married couple was not only an ancient fertility symbol, but also a way of luring evil spirits away from the marriage partners before harm could come their way.

9. If an owl hoots five nights in a row at a house while anyone is sick, it will probably cause them to die.

10. If you kill a snake in dry weather and want it to rain, hang the snake on a limb with its belly to the sun.

11. The number of white frosts in February indicates the number of frosts there will be in the following May.

12. It is bad luck to cut a baby's fingernails before it is a year old.

13. Thirteen is an unlucky number.

THE PULSE

The poet Robert Frost said that "the possibilities for tune from the dramatic tones of meaning struck across the rigidity of a limited meter are endless." What did he mean by that? For one thing, he is suggesting that poetry should be musical. And it is easy to tell from Frost's own poetry that *tune* doesn't necessarily mean pretty melody. Music, like poetry, can be harsh as well as pleasant. Frost also meant to imply that poems often use the music of dramatic voices of a persona or characters. By this time you have probably written so many narrative and dramatic poems using the voices of a variety of personae and characters that you know what Frost is talking about.

The last thing Frost mentions is *meter*. The richness and variety of music in poetry, he says, comes from casting voices across a set meter. So what is *meter*?

Pulse. Beat. Meter is the most regular kind of rhythmic pattern. A steady movement of accented syllables alternating with unaccented syllables often in this pattern: soft **loud** soft **loud** soft **loud**—like a heartbeat.

Read aloud this line from Frost's "The Housekeeper":

"It's you," she said. "I can't get up. Forgive me."

Underline the syllables that you say slightly louder; those are the accented syllables. Your marks will probably look something like this:

"It's you," she said. "I can't get up. Forgive me."

This line has eleven syllables—five unaccented syllables followed by five accented syllables, plus an unaccented syllable left over at the end of the line. If you want to get technical about it, you can call that metrical pattern *iambic pentameter*. An *iamb* is a single "soft **loud**" sequence of sounds (a**bout,** be**ware, e**nough**,** "It's **you**"), and there are five (*penta* = five) of them.

But you don't have to know technical terms to be able to write in patterns like this. You have probably been writing iambs in most of your writing, both poetry and prose, without knowing it, because this pattern is so natural to the way we speak and write.

Here is another excerpt from Frost's long dramatic poem, "The Housekeeper":

> "Haven't you seen him? Strange what set you off
> To come to his house when he's gone to yours.
> You can't have passed each other. I know what:
> He must have changed his mind and gone to Garland's.
> He won't be long in that case. You can wait.
> Though what good you can be, or anyone—
> It's gone so far. You've heard? Estelle's run off."

Get together with a couple of other writers/readers and have someone in your group read these lines aloud. Divide the poem and assign the first two or three lines to one person, the next two or three to another person, and so on. Now each of you should

1. count the syllables in each line;
2. mark the accented syllables.

Which of you found the line which doesn't have ten syllables?

Read the poem aloud again, emphasizing the accents you've marked. You will most likely disagree with each other; that's perfectly normal. The way you mark the meter will often be affected by the dramatic interpretation of the lines. Some readers will stress certain words; other readers will accent different ones. It doesn't matter whether you ever agree or not. Here is what does matter:

- The best poets, like Frost, often vary the metrical patterns they use. They allow for irregularities in the pattern so that the pulse or beat doesn't become too regular and monotonous.

- When you read metrical poetry out loud, you should read the lines naturally so that they sound like someone speaking. But underneath the voice you should sense, subliminally, the pulse, the beat of those accents undergirding the voice. That's what Frost meant when he spoke of "tones of meaning struck across the rigidity of a limited meter."

- Meter should never become obvious. This regular pattern of rhythm is like the girders of a building. After the construction is finished, you don't see the rigidity of steel holding up the building, though you know it's there.

YOUR PULSE

Go through your folder and read some of your drafts aloud, listening, as you go, for the pulse, the cadence of accents alternating with unaccented syllables in your words. It will be there, perhaps not always steady and regular, but since English is an accentual language (more so, say, than French) the rhythm and pulse *will* be there. When you find the draft that is more regular in its pulse than the others, mark the accented syllables.

Now try breaking the lines of this draft a new way—a line break after every five accents. Your lines will probably have ten syllables each, more or less. Check to see if that isn't so. Whether your lines are regular or irregular and rough, you can say that what you have now is iambic pentameter; and since your lines don't rhyme, you can also say your poem is in *blank verse,* if you want to get technical about it.

For centuries poets have written down voices and cast them in this five-beat line—Chaucer, Shakespeare, Milton, Browning, Tennyson, Frost. That's a good list to add your name to. There are other line lengths you can experiment with, too. For instance, if you want to try an eight-syllable, four-accent line, you'll be writing *tetrameter*. In any case, playing with patterns of rhythm in this way will give you endless possibilities for music in your writing. And you now know a new method of lineation, too.

FLASHING BACK

Riding my bike down Dry Creek Road, I become aware of two deerflies buzzing my ears. Above my gliding silhouette on the pavement, I watch their shadows circle my head like moons around a planet. I know better than to swat at one. They'll think that my arm is the tail of a horse and consider me fresh meat.

Once Michelle Simara and I canoed into a hatch of deerflies near an island on Reelfoot Lake. Before we knew what hit, the green-headed bloodsuckers had us covered. Michelle was screaming and I was waving the paddle in the air. Suddenly, we turned the boat over, held on to the sides and kicked toward open water, splashing a fog of flies as we swam. I watched a cooler full of baked chicken, apple pie, and Coke float off behind a beaver lodge. My plans for a romantic island picnic were ruined.

A jolt in the road jerks my bike wheel, and I slow down to stop at the turn onto Lickton Pike. I wonder what Michelle is doing now. That disaster happened twenty years ago. A stinging bite on my neck has me slapping and I speed toward home trying to outrun the flies.

This bike ride was yesterday. I hadn't thought about Michelle Simara in years. She was a thin Lake County girl with long brown hair and wide blue eyes. The mind is a curious organ. A physical stimulation like a buzzing fly sent me two hundred miles and a score of years into my personal history. Then my front tire hitting a pothole jarred me back to the present. Often, the voice in a poem flashes from present to past and then back again—as it does in this poem:

Internal Exile

My parents sit across from me, each with
A solemn and concerned look
Running across their faces . . .
A slightly guilty look.
"You've got to understand.
It's not you.
It's not you at all."

I turn sharply away
And gaze out the window
At the old oak,
Its branches swaying heavily in the wind,
The treehouse Dad and I built
Nestled safely in the branches.
Here are s'more nails, Dad! Lemme help!
I scrambled up the ladder of wooden boards
Nailed into the thick bark of the old tree.
Dad smiled around the nails in his mouth
As I struggled onto the platform.
He winked
And carefully placed the next nail.
The blows fell with a loud crack! Crack! Crack!

"Mark! This isn't easy for us either.
We know

How you must feel about this
And it's important for you to know
That it's not you.
It's us. Your mother and I.
We . . . have problems.
You know that . . .
You can hear us sometimes . . . "
He turns to Mom,
Looks away, clears his throat.
Mom looks from her
Hands
Fidgeting in her lap
To Dad, then to me,
And then to her hands again.
She is so good with them . . . gentle, kind, loving.

Every step was
A new lesson in pain.
My bigwheel lay on its side
At the bottom of the steep driveway.
I limped away, biting my lip,
(Blinking back the tears).
If only I can find Mom . . .
She'll make the pain go away . . .
WHERE IS SHE?
Oh Mark! What have you done to yourself?
Sit down, let me see, honey.
She carefully wiped the blood away,
And gently examined the gaping wound,
(A look of pain and hurt on her face
Each time I flinched).
Finally, with the knowing care
of all mothers,
Declared that my knee was going to live,
That I'd be all right.

"You'll be all right. It'll
Take some getting used to.
But I think it's the best thing
For all of us.
It might not even be forever . . .
Uh . . . right, Hon?"

She turns to Dad
With a look of sadness on her face,

Looks at me,
And gives a smile.
"Right, dear."

I know that it's forever.

—Matt Freeman

Now, read the poem again and find the sensory details that trigger the narrator's shift from present to past and back again.

The oak outside the window sends the persona back to the day he and his father built a treehouse. The "Crack!" of the hammer and the personal address "Mark!" bring him back to the room with his parents. His mother's gentle, loving hands remind Mark of the time when she comforted him after a childhood accident. Her pronouncement "That [he'd] be all right," is echoed by his father's "You'll be all right." Finally, the father's suggestion that the separation might not be "forever" is echoed by his son's certainty, "I know that it's forever."

All of us time-travel every day, every hour. It's so natural that we rarely stop to think about the unique powers of our brains.

Get a start by imagining that you are in another place—bedroom, kitchen, backyard, or someplace special just to you. See, smell, listen, and touch the place. Try to feel your presence there and start fast-writing. Discover where this leads you, what flashbacks occur.

LINE PATTERNS

So far, you've been breaking the lines of your poems at places where the meaning of your sentences tells you to pause—or at places where you wouldn't pause.

The visual appearance of your poem may also help you decide where to break lines. I find that much of the time I break lines so they are all more or less the same length. There is no reason for doing this other than a concern for the visual appearance of neatness. Once in a while, to prove to myself that I'm not stuck in a rut, I will arbitrarily choose to vary the length of lines rather drastically. Sometimes, as I write, I see a pattern emerging from the variety of line lengths; and I'll work to make that pattern or scheme more consistent. Here's an example:

New House

When I woke I knew this house
was not the bed and board, wall and roof of the past

twenty years. Numerous
times I have wakened
to borrowed bathrooms, stumbled into motel vanities,
staggered down alien
hallways, fallen short of the toilet, looked up startled
by mirrors on wrong
walls after midnight,
mirrors vanished altogether. But none of this coming to
discombobulated in houses
of momentary strangers, in the nervous, breathing
darkness of foreign bedrooms,

the drunken rooms of broken
friends, none of this waking, hither and yon, from sleep
sans rest had prepared me
for this bedroom swimming away from me into false dawn
burnishing the curtains
at 3:00 AM—the amber
security lamp in my new neighbor's backyard. Yet
no matter how estranged
and broken my mind believes I am, the bed I wake in
is familiar, and,
so, the woman beside me,
she who makes right any house, in any room of time,
in any darkness.

—M. G.

You figure out the pattern. Put down a series of letters, *S* for short lines, *L* for long, and see what you get. Is the pattern in the first stanza of fourteen lines related in any way to the pattern in the second stanza?

I set about breaking lines erratically and ended up turning the lineation into a pattern. That's the way the human minds works; it tries constantly to establish order. Let's say you had no idea why I broke my lines this way. You might decide the pattern could have some connection between the content and the form, between what is said and the way the poem is arranged on the page. Read the poem to someone and try to explain this connection.

Many poems are written to fit what seems like an arbitrary form or pattern. The simplest way of determining line length in a regular pattern, for example, is by having the same number of words in each line. Here is a poem written with line lengths determined by a word-count pattern.

The Tricyclist

The sidewalk thumps
under my wheels,
like train rails.

Sandspurs, sprigging from
the grass, chew
at the edges

of my tracks.
The world is
sunlight and leaves

in a long
swallow of wind.
Leaning, I take

the last corner
on two,
rock back to

three sure wheels.
I stop. My
front wheel touching

the garage door.
The wind dies.
I hold my

breath and
begin to
disappear.

                                        —M. G.

Patterns of this kind may seem to have nothing to do with the content or the tone or the meaning of the poem—at first. Once you have figured out the line-length pattern of "The Tricyclist," notice that the number of lines in each stanza form a pattern, too. Is the stanza length related in any way to the line length? And can you see how both of these patterns might be related to the subject and content of the poem?

In "New House" there may be a relationship between the speaker's talk about confusion and the erratic appearance of the line lengths, between the description of stumbling and staggering and the way the line breaks cause the reader to stagger down the page. The connection between the pattern and the content of "The Tricyclist" is a little more obvious and simplistic.

Take a recent draft, or a piece you wrote weeks ago, and experiment with the line lengths to see if a pattern emerges. Working at shape and pattern this way, seeing if you can fit what you want to say into a scheme of line length and stanza length, is an exciting challenge. And sometimes it will actually help you sharpen and improve your poem. It took me a long time to pare down "New House" so that the two stanzas mirrored each other; but in the process I made the poem more economical in places and gave it, perhaps, more subtlety and more impact, too.

Try revising a couple of drafts—one for visual effects of one kind or another, another to fit a word-count pattern that you invent. And keep in mind as you work that this kind of discipline is like a puzzle or game. Have fun as you go at it.

THE STATES OF SLEEPING AND WAKING

I was forcing wads of paper money into a Coke machine and they kept coming back out. I spread my fingers weblike trying to contain the flood of fives, tens, and twenties that erupted from the coin slot. It wasn't funny, I was desparate. Life on planet earth was somehow dependent on my success; the entire world was being flooded by this volcanic explosion of money. I jerked awake. My pulse was racing. Though I dreamed this a week ago, I can still feel the terrible sense of doom that surrounded me. I know this sounds ridiculous. Money doesn't erupt from a Coke machine like lava, but dreams are often strange and unexplainable.

Insomnia, dreaming, and waking are experiences all of us have during our lives. Some mornings we meet the day rested and happy. Other mornings we wake clouded and moody, haunted by the residue of dream images and feelings. Some nights we lie awake with little control over sleep. The next group of poems are about those strange states of mind associated with sleeping.

Not Knowing

Sometimes it's hard to get to sleep at night
not being able to remember
if I locked the door
and if the children have shut their bedroom doors
in case of a fire,

wondering if my daughter has forgiven me
for missing the recital
she practiced for all month.
I'm not able to shut my eyes
for feeling the cold, blue blood of Pastor McBride
pump through my veins,
thinking at any time
my breath too could stop
and I'd be with him there
lying on my back by the church altar.
It's difficult to get any rest at all
not knowing who has the bomb
or how big it is.
And I have doubts about the satellites
my children call stars
that float outside my bedroom window.
I wonder where their signals go at night
while I try to sleep,
eyelid fighting eyelid
not knowing if tomorrow
I will wake.

—Michele Gay

Insomniac

The night sky is only a sort of carbon paper,
Blueblack, with the much-poked periods of stars
Letting in the light, peephole after peephole—
A bonewhite light, like death, behind all things.
Under the eyes of the stars and the moon's rictus
He suffers his desert pillow, sleeplessness
Stretching its fine, irritating sand in all directions.

Over and over the old, granular movie
Exposes embarrassments—the mizzling days
Of childhood and adolescence, sticky with dreams,
Parental faces on tall stalks, alternately stern and tearful,
A garden of buggy rose that made him cry.
His forehead is bumpy as a sack of rocks.
Memories jostle each other for face-room like obsolete film
   stars.

He is immune to pills: red, purple, blue—
How they lit the tedium of the protracted evening!

Those sugary planets whose influence won for him
A life baptized in no-life for a while,
And the sweet, drugged waking of a forgetful baby.
Now the pills are worn-out and silly, like classical gods.
Their poppy-sleep colors do him no good.

His head is a little interior of grey mirrors.
Each gesture flees immediately down an alley
Of diminishing perspectives, and its significance
Drains like water out the hole at the far end.
He lives without privacy in a lidless room,
The bald slots of eyes stiffened wide-open
On the incessant heat-lightning flicker of situations.

Nightlong, in the granite yard, invisible cats
Have been howling like women, or damaged instruments.
Already he can feel daylight, his white disease,
Creeping up with her hatful of trivial repetitions.
The city is a map of cheerful twitters now,
And everywhere people, eyes mica-silver and blank,
Are riding to work in rows, as if recently brainwashed.

—Sylvia Plath

Sleep Falling

i jump off the Empire State Building,
riding the wind down until i hit the ground.
i see the floors slip by me, racing away like
all stolen dreams do in the dark gray smog.

guitar music fills the subways;
it's soothing underground, where hard lights
reveal only grim street faces.

i can't sleep, afraid i'll fall
back into some nightmare.
i stop to rest in my bed, hoping maybe
the sunrise will wait.

there's still some orange juice at the bottom
of the glass. i didn't drink it all.
i forgot.

someone chopped down the dead tree
out in the backyard.
i used to climb that tree when i was a kid.

but now, it's gone. someone i don't know
cut it down.

i'll hit the ground, if i fall asleep.
i'll die this time. only a few more feet left.
i feel the impact. the alarm clock rings.
everyone comes to sweep me off the pavement.
i can't get up.
the alarm clock continues ringing.

—J. H. Lee

Waking

The chatter of birds splashed the sky.
I woke. Then ebbed away
again on the thin tide of sleep.

Waking should be tried and final
like steel, swift as sparrows
breaking a border of trees.

But that morning I drowned
over and over, remembering
when you dreamed of me in her arms
and woke to cry alone, afraid to wake me.

—M. G.

Writing Ideas

Dreams are important sources for poetry. Notice that in the poems
you just read, the dreams are sometimes incoherent and illogical. You
will often find in dream poems free association of images and
metaphors; that's the way things happen in dreams. Details not connected in a logical, waking state are suddenly found together. The
effects created by this kind of association are strange and mysterious.
It's a subtle way to create a mood or atmosphere. Give it a try when
you write. Put down things as they come to you without worrying
about whether or not what you are saying makes sense.

1. In the poem "Insomniac," by Sylvia Plath, a man struggles to
    sleep in a night that has become strange and surreal. The stars are
    peepholes that partially cover "A bonewhite light, like death,
    behind all things." His pillow is a desert from which sleeplessness
    stretches "its fine, irritating sand in all directions." Sleeping pills

don't work. "Invisible cats / Have been howling like women, or damaged instruments." This poem, rich with horrible images and details, reveals how bad sleeplessness can be.

All of our sleeping habits are different. If you have experienced insomnia, try to recreate a sleepless, restless night.

2. Do you have recurring dreams? Is there one dream that stands out in your mind? Write a poem trying to capture the images, feelings, and atmosphere of the dream. You might include how the narrator feels after waking up. Don't have the person say, "Oh, I was only dreaming." That's been done too often. If you can't remember a dream, create one on the spot.

3. Have friends tell you their most unforgettable dreams—the best, worst, scariest, weirdest. Then fast-write about another person's dream. You might write this in first person as if it were your own or in third person as if you were an omniscient narrator.

4. Have you ever lain in bed and drifted in and out of consciousness? You might have been aware of light creeping in from the edge of the window or a dog barking in the neighbor's yard. Then you were in a dream again, or lost in sleep until you rose back to wakefulness like a bubble rising to the surface of water. Fast-write, trying to recreate a specific morning or night when you have had a similar experience.

SYLLABIC PATTERNS

As you've seen, there are a number of ways to set line length in a poem, and the length of the lines can become a pattern—determined by visual appearance on the page or by counting words per line. Here's yet another way: *syllabics*—line length set by the number of syllables.

The twentieth-century poet Dylan Thomas wrote a number of poems in stanzas that looked irregular but were actually highly organized patterns of syllabics. Here's the second stanza of his "Poem in October":

> My birthday began with the water-
> Birds and the birds of the winged trees flying my name
> Above the farms and the white horses
> And I rose
> In rainy autumn
> And walked abroad in a shower of all my days.

> High tide and the heron dived when I took the road
> > Over the border
> > And the gates
> Of the town closed as the town awoke.

Count the syllables in each line and write down the numbers for each line in a sequence. This will give you the line-length pattern Thomas uses in every one of the seven stanzas in this poem.

As you can see, by indenting the lines and centering (more or less) the very short ones, Thomas has also created a visual pattern pleasing to the eye. Whether or not there is any significant connection between form and content here I will leave to you to decide.

Working with a set line-length scheme of this kind can create—by accident—some interesting and often effective line breaks. Notice the way those short lines slow the poem down a little, at the point of the poem that the speaker is moving slowly as he gets up on a gray morning:

> And I rose
> In rainy autumn

Maybe Thomas planned for this effect; maybe he revised extensively so that it would work out this way; maybe he was simply lucky that it happened in his first draft. We'll never know. And it doesn't matter; in any case, the marriage between meaning and form works. You might want to go to the library and find a collection of Thomas's poetry. Read "Poem in October," checking to see how carefully he follows his stanza pattern, and to see if there are other places in the poem where content and form reinforce each other.

Now work on your own writing with an eye for lineation by syllabics. Take out an old draft and rewrite it, determining the length of the lines by syllable count.

You might make all your lines the same number of syllables, or you might vary the lengths, and then repeat the sequence in a set stanza pattern. You may have a logical reason for your pattern (you have a poem about football, so you work to make it eleven lines of eleven syllables each); or you may like the way the poem looks on the page; or you may create a scheme purely by whim. Do it any way you like, and keep in mind as you experiment that this kind of revising should be playful.

You may be surprised, when you get it all worked out, that you have improved your poem in several ways and that you have added some new dimensions to your work.

10

The Community of Writers–And Readers

By this time a writing community has probably developed in your class, with students talking about writing, sharing fast-writings, giving advice, complaining about writer's block. A writing community is an organized group that meets on a regular basis to share, give support, and critique so that each member's writing can be made more clear, inventive, and sharp. Sharing a new draft puts distance between the author and the writing, making revision easier.

I hope you've discovered that a good community of writers knows when to joke and when to be serious. In order to create good poems, poets must have the freedom to take risks. Taking risks often means revealing a vulnerable part of oneself, so an element of relaxed trust must develop among the members of a writing community.

In this chapter you'll need to rely on your writing friends to help you complete a collection of your best work. But before we get to that, we're going to knock out a few fast-writings and drafts about the class itself.

7:45 A.M., Writing Class

Morning sunlight evades the old steeple
of the First Baptist Church across the street,
falls through the dusty window panes on people
writing poems in Brown's room. At my feet,
girls in blue-jean jackets and loose t-shirts
sit together, laugh quietly. They share
intimacy with sunlight, the folds of their skirts

made as transparent as the strands of hair
hanging over their shoulders. Their presence
creates a gentle enchantment around
the room. I stare too long, and my conscience
begs me to work, to write, so I look down.

The atmosphere breaks with the bell's harsh ring
My tranquility dissolves, and I'm left with a poem about
    nothing.

                                                        —Ethan Pride

The Muse

Beside me
            your body moves so slowly,
            so naturally I can forget
            that you are there—
            head upon the table
            you mold into the room
and I sit
            upon the floor
            and look into the mirror,
            watch the reflected room,
            try to pull you out
            from among the vases
            and chair
here
            it would be easy for me
            to lose you,
            asleep you are like the soft rustling curtain
            which I can watch for hours
            but never see through
I could touch you now,
            wake you
            and you would open
            your eyes and come back
            and we would talk—
In the mirror
            the clock has stopped
            and your breathing is
            the only movement reflected

                                                    —Tamarie Spielman

Three Pencils at Frozen Head Creek

Tracy and Chris explore the moss-
covered rocks with pencils.
They find no lead point sharp enough
to follow the pattern of bubbles
that circles through the icy brook,
no modifier complex enough to describe
the swirling glint that roars
over lichen rocks,
no verb exact enough to render
the motion of so pure a movement.

Tracy chooses a single bubble
to follow through the rocks,
thinking how sad to be born in turbulent
beauty and have a life so short.
Chris traces a swaying shadow
to its green hemlock source
and wonders why the branch sways
in still air.

Tracy and Chris write:
they move pencils with the motion
of the hemlock,
words flow with the sound
of the brook.
They are the glimmer and roar.

—B. B.

These three poems were inspired by the writing community and place. In "The Muse" a student sleeping in the classroom becomes the inspiration for the poem. In "Three Pencils at Frozen Head Creek" the narrator blends what he imagines two students are writing with the natural beauty of a mountain creek.

The student poet of "7:45 A.M., Writing Class" starts with the city outside the classroom window, then follows the light inside. There he finds a delicate, sensual relationship between the sunshine and his classmates relaxing on the rug. This poem is written in a sonnet form. Even though the persona claims to have written a poem "about nothing," he captured the "gentle enchantment" of the writing class.

Think about the students in your class: friends, strangers, those whom you admire. Close your eyes and imagine a time when you found yourself watching them. Imagine the students writing, sleeping, or lost in thought. Let the lighting, the facial expressions, and the sounds in the room help create an atmosphere. Don't forget the paintings or posters on the wall. Capture a sense of the writing place with a fast-writing.

A BOUNCING COMMUNITY, OR CRITICAL MASS

Often while reading a friend's poem, I am struck with an idea, feeling, or image that inspires me to write. It may spark a memory or feeling that I need to explore. For some unknown reason, I might find a fictional character who has important words to tell. I might not even know the reason another person's poem makes me want to write. Sometimes a writing community is like an atomic reaction. Many poems bounce off each other, releasing an immense energy.

In the next poem a student reacts to other students' poems.

Hands

I am jealous of all you poets
that have rural grandmothers;
of all those poems
about their strong, old hands.

Every summer, I would fly to Florida.
Grandma would take me to Disney World.

There are schedules
in my grandparents' community.
Grandad plays golf
every Tuesday and Thursday.
He comes home mad,
but he says the Florida weather
is grand.

It is.
But I am always reading
of horse smells and rain falling
on a Virginia farm.

I wake up at night
hearing the wind
coming through the screened
condominium windows.
I lie there staring at their
pictures.

I see Grandma's hands
bent with arthritis,
clutching at a glass
of sun-brewed tea.

—Chris Sizemore

In "Hands" Chris expresses his jealousy, tinged with irony, for poets whose grandparents have "strong, old hands." While other students' grandparent poems reveal "Virginia farms" with "horse smells and rain falling," his memories are filled with Disney World and Florida weather. If he hadn't reacted to other students' writings, he might never have found his own grandparents' hands and this unique poem.

Here are some suggestions that may help you do your own bouncing:

1. If other students are always writing about experiences that don't fit your own, respond to them the way Chris Sizemore did. Be specific, fast-write.

2. Have each student choose a poem from his or her folder for other students to react to. Spend a class period sharing these poems out loud. Then post them on a wall so that they may be read silently. Bounce off each other's poems into fast-writings.

WORD MUSIC

The English language is rich in the music of word sounds. The variety of sounds in English gives a writer a rich palette of sounds and timbres to work with. And in English there is often a correlation between the meaning and the sound of words. Say the words *slow* and *quick* aloud and you'll see what I mean. Or try the words *happy* and *solemn*.

There isn't always a connection, but much of the time there is. Somber poems tend to sound somber, with long vowels and drawn-out consonants, such as *l*'s, *m*'s, *s*'s, and *n*'s. Poems about harsh subjects often have a high concentration of harsh sounds, like *t*'s, *k*'s, and *d*'s.

The following poem by Carl Sandburg is an example. Get into a group of at least three other people and read it aloud:

The Harbor

Passing through huddled and ugly walls,
By doorways where women haggard

Looked from their hunger-deep eyes.
Haunted with shadows of hunger-hands,
Out from the huddled and ugly walls,
I came sudden, at the city's edge,
On a blue burst of lake—
Long lake waves breaking under the sun
On a spray-flung curve of shore;
And a fluttering storm of gulls,
Masses of great gray wings
And flying white bellies
Veering and wheeling free in the open.

—Carl Sandburg

Assign the following four tasks to different members of your group:

1. Circle all of the harsh consonants and sounds.
2. Underline all of the smooth, pleasant sounds.
3. Put parentheses around the harsh, unpleasant, and cramped images.
4. Put brackets around the pleasant and expansive images.

Put your heads and books together and compare your markings. See if all (or most) of you agree about places where sound and meaning seem to go together well.

Question: Do you think Sandburg was consciously aware of these connections as he wrote, or as he rewrote, "The Harbor"?

You might take a look at other poems in this book to check this out further. Look for a poem that strongly expresses an emotion or mood, such as anger or sadness; then read the poem aloud to see if the sounds of the words echo the mood. You will find in some poems a stronger connection between sound and meaning than in others, but more often than not, sounds will reinforce meaning.

Now read aloud some of your own poems and drafts to see if there's a correlation between the music in your language and the subjects and moods of your work. Don't be surprised to find that you are a musical writer. Much of this musicality is built into the language and into our perception of it. The word *solemn* sounds serious and sad partly because of the long *o*, the drawn-out consonant sounds of the *s, l, m,* and *n,* and partly because from age three or so we have associated the meaning of *solemn* with the sounds that make up that word.

It shouldn't surprise you to find that the language you put down on paper comes back at you with spoken sounds that harmonize with the tone and meaning of your words. After all, people have been harmonizing with themselves in this way for centuries. The music of words is almost inescapable.

Question: Were any members of your group consciously aware of these connections as they wrote, or rewrote, their pieces?

And now for a response to the two questions above. It doesn't really matter whether or not writers are consciously aware of the word music they create. If the music is there, it's there; and there is no need to be concerned about how it came to be. Much of the time writers are not consciously aware of the music they make, though in revising they may develop an awareness of it. As you work on early drafts, you probably shouldn't think to yourself, "Hey, I think I need to sprinkle some alliteration in here"; there are too many other important things to occupy your mind in the early stages of getting a piece written. As you write, let the music happen naturally. When you revise later, you may refine and polish the word music.

YOUR OWN MUSIC

The best way to explore and develop your ear for word music is to *play* with sounds; and the best way to do that is by letting your sense of logic and meaning go to sleep, so to speak. And the best way to do that is to write nonsense.

In other words, concentrate on letting sounds bounce off each other, echoing and contrasting. Don't worry about *what* you are saying; don't even think about making sense.

I wrote the following poem by sitting down at the typewriter and letting my mind go blank. Then I typed whatever came into my head, letting the music of the words lead me where it would. Read the poem aloud. But keep in mind that it's the kind of poem that refuses to allow a reader to "tell it back." Don't try to make "sense" of it; just listen and flow with the music.

Wiggins Winker Slot

Wiggins winker slot
eye slipper finger
thumb the taste of
edgy blood. Wiggins

broken toe and knee
cripple happy twisting
rope. All root and
stubble grit the nail

stumping carpet straw
and berry. Wiggins
strum the rhubarb
thumbnails splicing

sternum. Holy gutting
cranks the tendons
corded bristle veins.
Wiggins leaping wink-

ing thickening the
shine. Knock and wait
and knock the door all
keyed all ache and

grip. Wiggins rip the
laces sky and lava throw
mountain fall the star
back broken over rivers.

—M. G.

I warned you it would be nonsensical. There are places in this poem where the syntax and grammar are ambiguous; that is, some words can function as two parts of speech at once. Is *fall* in the next-to-last line a noun modified by the adjective *mountain,* or is it a verb whose object is *star?* I say it doesn't matter: read it either way; read it both ways. Ambiguity is often a powerful tool for poets, allowing them to say two things at once. In any case, I wrote this piece for music, not grammar.

And although "Wiggins Winker Slot" doesn't seem to *mean* or *say* anything, it may still communicate—a mood, a tone, if nothing else. How would you describe the mood of this poem?

Many nonsense poems are written in a stanza pattern, often with rhymes, probably because the mind, having abandoned the usual logical sequence of thoughts, needs to establish some sense of order. Or it may be that such poems take us back to the nursery rhymes of our earliest childhood. Here is another nonsense poem, a lullabye— ironically, not for a child, but for a mother:

County Lullabye
For My Mother

Speak me your fitful firstlight,
even cockshut light,
purple groundlight,
under far trees.

Tell me your greening bonelight,
slanting rocklight,
falling stormlight,
ruddy as flame.

Word me your winging windlight,
nodding flowerlight,
in winging windlight,
fallow and blue.

Cry me your hollow lealight,
towering hill-light,
swagging southlight,
in beading rain.

Breathe me your beaming treelight,
dipping boughlight,
dripping twilight,
drupelet and pome:

Your many-mirrored
musters of pit-flesh:
apple and berry,
berry and plum.

Sing me your spinning streamlight,
shivering shoal-light,
level calmlight,
after the whelm.

And let your song be
profulent as water,
chequered as treechange
changing color:

grassemerald, stumpdark,
boughblanched, hillheavened.
And let your song be
as soft and simple

as quavering sickcall,
childcall whispering
I am afraid.
And let it be hands

bright as small lanterns
facing the housedark,
five tender glosses
appearing approaching

doubling, redoubling.
And let it be sleep,
sleep now, my little one,
hush now, sleep.

—George Scarbrough

Read both of these poems again and notice how consonants are repeated (alliteration) and how vowels are repeated and echoed (assonance). And when the last syllable(s) of a word (the final consonant and the vowel that precedes it) matches the last syllable(s) of another word, there's a rhyme, of course. That happens quite often in Scarbrough's poem, though technically rhymes involving the same word (such as *light* in "County Lullabye") are called *identities*.

Here is a poem written by a student after hearing Scarbrough's poem. Notice that she begins with a line from a nursery rhyme and then quickly takes off on her own:

Nonsense Poem

ashes to ashes
dust to dust
circle
round and round
infallible cycle
more dependable than the Postal Service
    life into death
        into . . . what?
    life again
stepping from stone to stone
            only to stop at start
green halted by red
        warned by yellow
            caught by flashing blue

rule and law stifle individual
    puts a spiked collar on the brain
    and leads it by a short leash
removing a band-aid rips
    every hair from its follicle
it hurts to heal

       —Millie Fly

Writers of nonsense poems often find that writing for word sounds leads them to make up new words to create the music they want. Here is an excerpt from such a nonsense poem:

Blue Hum Ramble

Walking the grumby and humfallen sidewalks
along my namby-panky neighborhood, I stummed
and fammled in my dringy, hapstruck brain
hows I didn't have a drim of an idea where
it was I was maundering and skilfing to.

       —Chris Bowman

Write your own nonsense poem. Or several. Forget trying to make sense. Often your poem will give you a kind of sense you hadn't been looking for. Or readers will find it for themselves. Don't worry about it one way or another; concentrate instead on *playing* with the word sounds. This is one time that you probably should be aware of the music you're making as you write. Bounce sounds off each other. Rhyme, if you like; that's certainly a kind of music. You may not end up with a top-notch poem; but then you might. In any case, the practice you do and the musical sensibilities you develop will affect other pieces you write.

BOUNCING II

Poets not only gain inspiration from other writers, but from other artists in the visual arts, dance, and music. The possible writing ideas generated by other art forms are limited only by the scope of your imagination. The following poems reveal just a few.

Pink and Blue A Cappella

Georgia O'Keeffe
has a painting of music—

not notes on a staff,
but an adagio
in pink and blue.
I saw it at the
Metropolitan Museum of Art,
and I only wish
that it were bigger.
I wish that it were big
and spherical and I
could curl up inside it
like a baby in the womb
listening to the thump
of its mother's heart
and the swish
of the amniotic fluid,
rolling to sleep
in the midst of waves
of pink and blue
like the first music,
the music that was my mother.

—Travis Loller

Nighthawks

2 A.M.
in the diner
she sits alone
lapping lukewarm coffee
like mother's milk
from a caffeine-stained cup
pale blue flowers
chipped from the rim
I look
down the counter
past her left ear
to the clock
on the faded grey wallpaper
then down at my watch that stopped
hours ago
my own coffee black
deep
swirling with the nervous
touch of my spoon

I watch her for a moment
obviously not watching me
she is caught in the whirlpool of her coffee cup
I drown myself in mine.

—Stephanie Lydick

Living Dead
from Van Gogh's
"skull with a burning cigarette"

Collar bones and vertebrae,
ribs and rounded skull,
exposed teeth no longer hidden,
maybe making a grin
—you have been this all along.
We imagine the rest.

Only now you can hang back
and watch us all follow your steps
performing the lives we have left.

You have opened eyes
and no longer sleep,
living dead
(dead but living),
brought down to your basics,
your substance,
your structure,
sharp and animate in the curves
of the jaw and cranium.

You can sit down
and relax with a cigarette
and smoke happily
because you have no lungs.
Bare, skinned, and unclogged:
life itself passes through you
more easily now.

—John Post

Jazzman

The jazzman plays—
rumpled suede coat

and zoot pants
but man, there's the shirt
purple—same shade driving—
coasting down the Sierras,
clutch in.

Jazzman tries a new angle
throws his back to the wind
trying to catch the violet
on the wind where it belongs
back to the atmosphere
so it can slither down
like only silk can
into my red eyes
wishing for a deeper shade.

                              —Max Otterland

An Accusation
(from a photo-essay on the homeless)

Yes, I know you.

I look at you through
the black and white picture frame
that imprisons me,
staring at your body
held tensely.

I've seen you turn away
from my patchwork house,
made of bits of wood,
tarp, and metal.

You stare at your leather tennis shoes,
when my children walk past
in scraps of clothing,
as raggedy as the shelters
we live in.

You fumble with your bookbag,
and tighten it.
Your hands grasp
for something to do,
eyes desperately
seek another focus,
so you can politely turn away,

and pretend not to see
my shadowy shape.

Yes I know you,
sitting there underneath my photograph,
examining the lighting and lines
of the picture,
trying your best
to stare past
my tightly focused eyes.

—Vanessa Cain

To Monsieur Seurat

You envision a leisurely Sunday in the park
as a chemical mixture
of vivid colors

each leaf on your tree
is made of
        tiny molecules
of green
        with nuclei of sour yellow;
bright red electrons
        swirl
        like the river's current
in a lady's upright parasol,
        her regal stance
attributed to a backbone of
        stiff navy atoms;
hundreds of starchy white protons
combine to form
        stiff white sails
(on synthetic wooden masts)
        filled
with transparent neutrons of wind

You are, Monsieur Seurat,
a chemist of colors
        masquerading

—Millie Fly

You could spend a few days on these ideas—or weeks. First make
a list of your favorite works of art: visual arts, music, dance, crafts.
This might include work by friends and family. Do you remember a

day spent at a gallery, a concert, ballet, or a poster you have on your bedroom wall? Pick a specific memory and fast-write the specific event, revealing your experience.

The members of your writing community should bring art and photography books to class. Ask your librarian to help you choose some books you can check out to the writing place. Spread the books out on tables. Then browse. Find an art work that you react strongly to. If ideas start coming, fast-write.

Here are a few approaches suggested by the student models:

1. The narrator of "Pink and Blue A Cappella" describes her emotional response to a painting by Georgia O'Keeffe. Though the painting is static, the poem reveals rich sound, texture and motion. Words like *womb, thump,* and *swish* help the reader feel the sensual nature of her experience through image and word sound. Let the color, texture, and brush strokes of a painting carry you with them. Let the fast-writing become the experience.

2. In the poem "Nighthawks," two people are drinking coffee at the counter of an all-night diner. They are separated by more than the space between them. "The faded grey wallpaper" and the narrator's "own coffee black / deep / swirling with the nervous / touch of [her] spoon" help to create an atmosphere that is lonely, bleak, and anxious. The poet wrote about this painting from the inside out. Become a character in a painting. Reveal the atmosphere and the story that you feel the work implies.

3. In "Living Dead" the narrator speaks to the skull in Van Gogh's painting as if it were alive. Comic irony is created when the persona tells the skull, "You can sit down / and relax with a cigarette / and smoke happily / because you have no lungs." Have a conversation with a person, animal, or object in a painting. Talk to the painting itself. Try for comedy or irony if it feels right.

4. "Jazzman" is a whimsical poem that describes a jazz musician in performance. Recall a specific concert or ballet. Write about the performance. Be sure you include details like the physical relationship between a musician and his instrument. Write freely. Let your imagination find unusual comparisons, like the jazzman playing, " . . . driving— / coasting down the Sierras, / clutch in."

6. "An Accusation" was written by a student after she viewed photography that documented the plight of the homeless. Her narrator is one of the homeless in a photograph. The persona is speaking to the writer, a person interested in photography who has come to see the show: "Yes I know you, / sitting there underneath my

photograph, / examining the lighting and lines / of the picture, / trying your best / to stare past / my tightly focused eyes." Have a person in a painting, sculpture, or photograph speak directly to you or to other spectators.

7. The poem "To Monsieur Seurat" speaks directly to the artist. The narrator uses specific details from the painting to prove that the painter is "a chemist of colors / masquerading." Directly address the artist of a painting or a piece of sculpture.

8. Have you ever watched an artist at work? Describe a potter throwing a pot, a wood-carver shaping a bird, a sculptor discovering a face in stone, a weaver forming a rug in the colors of a desert sunrise, or a painter brushing a canvas. Try to include tools, materials, the motion of the hands and body, and the artist's facial expressions.

MORE MUSIC

The English languge is rich in the music of word sounds, and you have already experimented a bit with repeating and echoing vowels (assonance) and consonants (alliteration). Another kind of music available to writers in English is *rhyme*—matching vowels and following consonants (if there are any) at the ends of words. You may have wondered why the subject of rhyming has not been mentioned in this book until now, and why we suggested, back in the "Introduction to the Teacher," that beginning writers should avoid rhyme until they had written a sizable body of work. Now you're going to find out, at last.

Most people think rhyming in English is easy. It *is* easy to rhyme—in the singsongy style of nursery rhymes. But rhyming with subtlety and sophistication is quite difficult. The reason? English is actually rhyme-poor, in comparison with some of the Romance languages like Spanish and Italian.

In the beginning, English poets structured their verse using patterns of repeated sounds at the beginnings of words (alliteration, or head rhyme, as it is sometimes called). Those Anglo-Saxon poets knew instinctively that the real strength and music of the English language lay in those consonants. A few centuries later, when English came under the influence of the cultures in Europe, poets in England decided they should follow the models of poets writing in French and Italian, so they began to use rhyming and patterns of rhymes in established schemes (such as sonnets, rondels, sestinas, villanelles).

The French language is rich in vowel sounds and has fewer distinct and hard consonant sounds—such as *t, k, d, b,* and *p*—at the ends of words. French seems to be richer in possibilities for rhyme than English, and not quite so limited by the final consonants; and the same might be said of the Italian and Spanish languages.

Rhyming in English is often more restricted and difficult. If a poet uses the word *life* in a villanelle, for instance, that long *i* + *f* syllable must be matched at least six times. And what are his choices? *Rife, strife, knife, wife.* This poor writer won't be able to write what he really wants to say; those rhymes are going to force him to write a poem about a home life so rife with strife he'll be driven to taking a knife to his wife.

Writing in a language that is rhyme-poor means that you are going to be stuck with the same sounds that thousands of poets in the past have been stuck with, and originality may be more than a challenge—it may be nearly an impossibility. If you use *tune* as a rhyme word, get ready for cries of "Cliché, cliché!" from your fellow writers and your readers, because you're likely to come up with rhymes we've all heard before, like *croon, June, moon.*

Rhyming also encourages writers to write empty and trite phrases to help them get that rhyme sound or to get a line of poetry to stretch out to the rhyme sound needed at the end:

> I'll never, no, never, no, never forsake.

So ends the last stanza of a nineteenth-century hymn. I suppose one could argue that repeating "no never" is a way of being emphatic, but I suspect the writer may have simply run out of gas and repeated himself emptily to finish out the line. Repetitions of this sort are no great sin, of course; and in a song or a hymn, writers can more easily get away with the commonplace. But a writer of serious poems shouldn't spoil an otherwise original and perhaps emotionally powerful piece of writing with the trite or the silly. Songs are often learned not from written music but by word-of-mouth, and rhymes are useful as mnemonic devices, ways to help the singer remember the lines. Poetry is a different art form, and readers of poetry are likely to expect more subtlety.

Rhyme is only one kind of word music available to a poet. Like other kinds, rhymes should remain almost subliminal so that they have their effect without becoming noticeable or interesting in themselves. You don't want your reader to become intent on listening for that rhyme (like the bell at the end of the typewriter carriage) so that he misses what you're saying.

So how do poets make rhyme sounds subtle? At the beginning of this section I said that rhyming is difficult. It is, but here are some tricks to make sophisticated rhyming easier:

1. Choose rhyming words that offer you plentiful choices. You can check off the possibilities in your head, or check in a rhyming dictionary. Avoid rhyming with words like *breath*, for example. All you have is *death*.

2. At least some of the time you might try choosing small and insignificant words so that the rhymes won't be too obtrusive or noticeable. I once wrote a poem using rhyming words like *if, and, it,* and *from*—partly to make sure the rhymes wouldn't call much attention to themselves, and partly as a challenge—just to see if I could do it.

3. Enjambment is the most important technique you can use to mute and disguise rhymes to make them less obvious. End-stopping lines in a rhymed poem only makes the rhyme sounds stand out more obviously. By enjambing your lines, you will place the sound at the end of the *line*, but you will lose it in the middle of the phrase or clause so that readers won't emphasize it as much as they would if it appeared at a major pause in the sentence (such as at a period, semicolon, or comma).

Read the next poem aloud to someone who hasn't read this part of the book yet:

Eighty
   —for my father's eightieth birthday

I hated guns and couldn't hit a can
with a .22 at twenty paces. Baseball
statistics and the game always ran
first and second on my list of all-
time yawning bores, and while my earnest friends   5
fielded flies in the suffocating sun,
I swam a one-mile lake from end to end
or pounded cinders at night in a 3K run.

I'll hike a rocky ridge, but stay back
a few breaths from the cliff. I say, Good   10
for them, those brave men who dance their fears
by leaping from planes, with thin cloth in a pack
their only salvation.

My father has well understood
what I have said here for nearly eighty years.

—M. G.

After you have read the poem aloud, ask your listener whether or not it rhymes. See if the listener can tell you any of the rhyming sounds.

Your listener may have caught a few of the rhyme sounds, such as the ones in the end-stopped lines (sun / run); but I hope he or she didn't find them more interesting than the content of the poem. If the listener didn't think the poem rhymed at all, I'd be pleased, because I'd rather have the music of the rhyming affect him or her at a subliminal level, like the other kinds of word music in the poem.

MUSIC PATTERNS

Reread "Eighty" above. Now label the rhyme in that poem with letters of the alphabet, marking the first rhyme sound *a*, the next *b*, and so on. Whenever a rhyme appears, label it with the same letter you used the first time you labelled it.

If you come out with a string of letters like this

a b a b c d c d   e f g e f g

you got it right. That series of letters is the rhyme scheme for that poem.

When I use rhymes, I usually let the scheme or pattern of rhymes evolve as I go, so that the form of the poem is growing naturally out of the content. I also write poems knowing in advance what the rhyme scheme will be. I can make up a pattern of my own or use a scheme invented by someone else, perhaps centuries ago. The sonnet is such a pattern that evolved in Italy in the Renaissance. It is hard to pull off in English because it requires you to repeat the first two rhyme sounds four times, rather than just twice:

a b b a   a b b a   c d e   c d e

Another version of the Italian sonnet makes it even more of a challenge with only two rhyme sounds in the last six lines:

a b b a   a b b a   c d   c d   c d

Poets in English developed their own brand of fourteen-line scheme:

a b a b   c d c d   e f e f   g g

They called this a "sonnet." It's a bit easier since it allows you to

change rhyme sounds more often, thus avoiding the problem of finding word sounds that have to be repeated three or four times.

Which pattern did I use in "Eighty"?

Right. Neither one. It is actually a blend of the two kinds of
sonnets: the first eight lines are in the English pattern; the last six, in
the Italian. And to tell the truth I can't remember whether or not I
decided I would follow that scheme before I began. It doesn't matter,
but I suspect I started out to write an English sonnet and found,
two-thirds of the way along, that the poem was handing me rhymes
in a different pattern. Maybe I got to line 11 and couldn't find a word
to rhyme with *back* in line 9. I had written *fear* at the end of 11 and
suddenly realized, perhaps, that I could finish with another c d e
pattern. You might say I cheated. Or you could just as easily say that
forms in poetry have always evolved this way. You *could* say I
invented a brand new kind of sonnet.

Whenever a poet writes in a form or pattern like this, it becomes
a kind of game. The trick is to play the game within all the boundaries
and limitations of whatever form you are using (or evolving) without
compromising your content (any more than you have to). The challenge is to say what you would have said without any set form, but to
do it within the confines of the form, without letting the form push
you around and lead you to say things you don't want to say because
they aren't true to your way of thinking or saying.

Go back and read the first poem in this chapter, "7:45 A.M., Writing Class." Label the rhyme sounds and then check to see if it is an
English or Italian sonnet. Notice that one of Ethan's rhymes is not
quite exact (*around / down*). Rhymes that are close but not exactly the
same are *slant rhymes*. For the first few sonnets you write, give yourself a little latitude once in a while when choices get tough. It is better
to fudge a little now and then to avoid choosing a rhyme that forces
you to say something you don't want to say, or in a way you wouldn't
usually write it. After you've written a dozen or so poems in set
forms, you can get tough with yourself and become a purist about
such technical things.

Likewise, you probably shouldn't worry too much about line
length this early in the game. Traditionally, sonnets are written in
iambic pentameter. (Check chapter 9, the section entitled "The Pulse,"
if you've forgotten what that is.) For your first few sonnets you might
try for ten syllables (more or less) per line. That will put you in the
neighborhood of that five-beat line.

Check Ethan's sonnet again. This time pay particular attention to
the way he enjambs lines. The periods that end his *sentences* often
come in the middle of his *lines*. Major pauses like periods or commas

don't occur at the ends of lines. The reader moves off the rhyme sound quickly to get to the next line, so that rhyme sound isn't emphasized.

Now read these two poems: "Confirmation," by Katye McCullough (chapter 4) and "Sonnet for the Blend of Music and Nature," by Tamarie Spielman (in "A Sample Chapbook," which follows this chapter). Check to see if they followed the three suggestions for subtle rhyming listed above in the section "More Music."

Now you should be ready to play this game yourself. Use any of the sonnet rhyme schemes, or use my version. (What should we call it, "Englian"?)

You are used to writing narrative and descriptive poems by now, so you might describe a scene, as Ethan did in "7:45 A.M., Writing Class," and as Tam did in "Sonnet for the Blend of Music and Nature." Or you might want to tell a story in your sonnet. Organizing the content of a narrative or descriptive poem will be second nature to you, and you will be able to concentrate on getting the rhyme scheme to work out right.

THE CHAPBOOK

At the beginning of chapter 10, we said that you would complete a collection of your best poems. Now is the time to start. First browse through your folder of finished work and select possible drafts to consider for inclusion. Begin by ordering poems chronologically by chapters. This will give you a view of your total progression of work and help you resist the temptation to use only your last poems without first considering others. Choose about twelve to fifteen of your best works to include in the first brief collection of your poems in a chapbook (a small book of poems or prose pieces).

Here are some suggestions that might help you arrange your book:

1. You might find that in ordering your poems by the chapters in this book, an inherent sequence already exists. Individual lives, journeys, and years have beginnings, middles, and endings. Chronology is the most obvious method, time-honored and true.

2. Group your poems by related subjects, themes, moods, or images.

    a. Subjects: Students have often selected a group of poems that was related in some way to a specific subject. These poems have been as varied as a canoe trip in Canada, a place (house, neighborhood, town), a valuable friendship, animals and pets, or a divorce. You probably won't have an entire book about one subject, but sections of the book can be grouped by subject.

b. Themes: This is closely related to subject. You might have written poems about the subjects childhood and young adulthood. Together these could represent the theme of growing up, of personal maturation. In this case, you may be ordering your chapbook by chronology as well as by theme.

c. Moods: All of us have poems that are sad, angry, happy, confused, mean, funny, or a combination of several moods. Often the characters we create to narrate poems undergo an experience that creates or springs from a mood. These shouldn't be hard to recognize. You might group poems similar in mood and/or arrange them for contrast.

d. Images: One of my student's collections is about growing up in India. Many of his poems contain images that are part of that setting: peacocks, rickshas, rice fields, saris, and bazaars. These images so dominated his poems that he gave his collection the title *Peacocks*.

Another student discovered that many of her poems contained images of flying. Even though her subjects and moods were different, she was able to use the common image of flying to help tie dissimilar poems together.

3. Juxtapose and contrast: a musician once told me that when he was arranging songs for a new album, he tried to vary tempo and mood. This made each song stand out in his listeners' minds.

Project an audience of readers out there. Vary mood, length, and subject so that your book will constantly surprise.

4. Begin and end with your strongest poems. Catch your readers' attention and leave them at the end satisfied but wanting more. Perhaps the first and last poem might somehow be related, which will help frame your book—like many good poems.

5. When you start, it is hard to hold all your poems in your head. A handy way of organizing them is to find a wall or table where you can spread them out to see them all at once. Spend several days making possible groupings.

Arranging a small book of poems is, in some ways, like writing a poem. You should feel free to edit as you work on your arrangement, eliminating poems (one or maybe several) that don't fit into your scheme very well.

You might be too close to your own poems to see some vital relationships, so call on the members of your writing community for help. Before you make final decisions about the design of your book, ask friends and teachers whom you trust to make suggestions about possible groupings or changes in your arrangement. You don't have to take their advice, but you might find their ideas helpful.

When you have worked out the best order for your chapbook, you need to think of a title. Here are some ideas to help you:

1. Use the title of your lead or closing poem as the title of the book.
2. Use the title of a poem that has a theme central to all of your work.
3. Use a dominant subject, image, theme, or mood as your title.
4. Use a key phrase from one of your poems, a phrase that suggests the theme or mood that predominates in your work.

Other students and writers have come up with titles such as these:

The Balance of Things	by Rebecca Bice
Motorcycles on the Wall and Selected Poems	by Michael David Woolf
Losing Innocence	by Janice Moore
ten poems to read with coffee a tiny book	by Max Otterland
Peacocks	by Anoop Singh
Through the Woodworks	by John Post
standing faceless atop a flaming mushroom	by Joyce Wilson

The final step is the actual printing of your book. You may type your poems and put them in a binder. (Calligraphy might be a substitute for typing, if you or someone you know can do a first-class job of it.) If you have access to a word-processor that can set type or a xerox machine that will reduce the size of your typed pages, you might make a book $5^1/2$ by $8^1/2$ inches. Place the poems side by side on pieces of paper $8^1/2$ by 11 inches and xerox the pages. (You'll have to make up a dummy, a trial layout of your book, so that you will know which poems go on which sides of the sheets of paper. Then fold and staple or bind along the fold.

However you print and lay out your book, you will probably want to xerox a number of copies to give to your family and friends.

A SAMPLE CHAPBOOK

Before you get started on your own chapbook, read the following collection of poems put together by the student Tam Spielman. Following her ten poems, she explains the process she followed in selecting and ordering them.

Currents

A Chapbook
by
Tamarie Spielman

The Muse

Beside me
        your body moves so slowly,
        so naturally I can forget
        that you are there—
        head upon the table
        you mold into the room
and I sit
        upon the floor
        and look into the mirror,
        watch the reflected room,
        try to pull you out
        from among the vases
        and chair
here
        it would be easy for me
        to lose you,
        asleep you are like the soft rustling curtain
        which I can watch for hours
        but never see through
I could touch you now,
        wake you
        and you would open
        your eyes and come back
        and we would talk—
In the mirror
        the clock has stopped
        and your breathing is
        the only movement reflected

Defining Terms (in my mother's voice)

You are heavy upon my back,
like a sack of potatoes.
As I weed the garden,
pick the green bananas
from the stalk in front
to store under the house
until they fade yellow
in the warm Hawaii twilight,
your weight constantly reminds me
I have a child.
Sometimes in the night
I wake afraid it is only
some firm dream—
the 36 hour labor, the sharp birth pains
almost caesarean, then your
wide, bright eyes warming me
like the Pacific currents you play in.
I like to think how similar we are—
both allergic to the same pink-white
tree blossoms of the plumeria,
both growing closer until
I think maybe we will be one again.
I will send you to preschool
though I could be your playmate forever—
some day you will be grown
and my term will really end.
Then when you drift
from me it will be your own motion
which will carry you,
and though my muscles
will tighten, I will be still.
These pains are deeper, quieter,
emptier but just as natural.
For a while longer
you will let me carry you
strapped to my back as I work.
I can feel you
growing heavier every day.

Melted Prints
—for my sister Kel

You think that
I am the big sister,
that you are always
behind me as we walk
through the earthen
forest path
and that while
I go through
the trees I
hold the branches
for you.
You gather the
leaves as they fall
from my shoulders.
In the winter
when the trail
is snow covered
you try to put your feet
after mine in
the deep melted prints.
But in the quick
shift to night
you don't see me
slip swiftly behind,
follow close
through the edge
of twilight
squeezing myself
into your shadow.

Esprit De Bois
   (*for Gervais Annecy*)

It was Thursday when I walked
down from the waterfall rocks,
where I ate my lunch of baguette and cheese,
on the small country road
which passed across your land.
The land your family had farmed since the 1500's,
where your sons and grandsons
baled the hay before it rained.
I can remember seeing you
first from up the road—
a funny old man with a hat,
sitting on the tired
wooden steps of his chalet
waiting for people to pass,
face wrinkled into a smile.
Perhaps I was the first one in weeks
to stop and talk to you.
You took me through your vegetable garden,
beyond the flower-encircled house
to the woodshed, dusty and ancient.
I watched your hands as we walked—
worn smooth and calloused from your work.
Inside you showed me
how you made the seille
for carrying potatoes or milk,
told me that you and your father
had made all the tools.
You had carved a self-portrait
in your work bench—
a young man with a smile.
You were so pleased to have your picture taken
with your wood, the closest you could be
to your family's past.
As I left, your wife came out
and stood with you.
I was probably the last person

to stop at your steps,
to really see your hands—

Today, Gervais Annecy, they found you in your field
where you had been cutting a path
with your scythe through the grass
so your wife could go to morning mass
without getting her feet wet.
You lay on your back as though resting,
face smiling up
like a carving on the earth.

6 Autumn Days

many apples,
not red but
yellow red,
that still have
their stems and
leaves, in a
new bowl
beside the
board-worn
window sill

the small november
waterfall looks
the same as
in may
only the water moves
as if it knows
the month
by the leaves
which cling to it

strands of hair
blowing on
a barbed-wire fence

a leaf, shadow
cast upon the
creek bottom,
slowly floating
into the shade

the sun bobs
along the water
as unsinkable
as a fallen
acorn top

a shriveled leaf,
fall-touched,
upon a rock
waiting
palm open

the branch
swaying as if
the heavy weight
of winter
lies upon it
in the still air

Sonnet for the Blend of Music and Nature

From the tree a dark shadow lifts, the thrum
of bird wings plucked like the soft mandolin
strings you play beside me. Chrysanthemums
lie faded beneath fall leaves and the flint
colored sky brings winter thoughts. Somewhere loons
fish freezing waters and mahogany
brown earth ices hard. But I'm most attuned
with this place today, for Calliope
lies in the hills chanting in the slanting
winds around us, calling winter. You draw
notes from your fingers which echo the span
of the lake and settle upon the spawn
fungus and the russets. The wind lightens
and your song mingles with the winter wren's.

Currents

Tonight I stand beside the river,
lose myself in its constant moving sounds.
They rush into the darkness,
fill my eyes with pictures of the way
it looks. There is no question in my mind
that if I run suddenly through the dark forms
I know as trees, trip over the rocks
at the edge and dive trustingly forward,
the chill waters will catch me, pull me in fast
and draw me deep downstream.

I just take this on faith—
that you know me well enough to see
in my eyes when I'm afraid,
and that you will be there
to watch the sunrise with me.
Why must I explain, define things
like the twisted tree we saw hiking today,
hollowed, stretching empty off the hill,
spiralling toward the river, its branches
reaching toward sky. I watched
it, wanting to see it grow.

Tomorrow morning we will dip our heads
in the water to wash our hair, and it
will pound cold winter on us
drawing away the warmth of other seasons.
On the way home we will watch
pools of dark birds sweep through the sky
southward more swiftly than we can drive,
drawn by an unseen current.

We feel the pull too, deep inside
where we never ask.

Strong Hold

All week in the water
doing laps, using all strokes
out to the island and back,
we practiced life-saving
until the struggle
with a drowning person seemed natural,
all panic carefully worked out
like rubbing away a cramp.
Use the water, don't fight it,
they told us. Let it help move you,
imagine the ripples
as extensions of your hands.
So, we leaned into our strokes,
sank our arms in with urgency
and embraced the liquid, relaxed
into its simple hold on our lives.

But tonight the water awakens,
arms of the storm shake it to fury.
I watch the lake like a cat
arch its back to the rain,
ripples shimmering like claws.
Above the water, lightning
forces its sharp form toward shore,
fingers reach through the trees
beckoning to me—
come swim, you have much to learn.

The Hermit Sees Himself in the World Around Him

I walk the trail
which winds into the forest.
The stream has begun
to gather leaves
and hold broken branches and sky—
water sifts under
the reflections smoothly,
swaying the trees.
The cabin will be waiting
with its soft wooden creaks.
The air around me rustles,
everything holds the susurrous colors
of mountain life.

People creak differently—
the sounds of breathing,
hands crumbling dirt,
the sliding of skin, a pen.
Living alone I hear myself
in the morning breeze
and the woven spider's web which breaks
against my face as I walk through it.
Sometimes in the night
I hear the sounds of stillness,
nothing is ever totally quiet,
emptiness is only a place
we block off from ourselves.
When I reach the cabin
there will be no one.
I will bring my shuffling inside
and close the door.

Tension

1

There is a leaning feeling when you walk downhill
a long way. At first your body
tries to compensate, longs for the upright balance,
scared of the forward momentum.
But eventually you stretch your legs
further and further, take longer strides
and lean into them, strain to relieve the tension
of holding back.

2

Imagine Chinese water torture. Anticipate
each drop touching your forehead,
slowly. Bead by bead a pull is created,
an unrelieved stress.
I can feel it too
when I watch clouds move in, crawl over the hills,
hazing the trees. Lightning stabs,
sparks across the sky
and I wait for the rain.
I become attached to each drop,
a part of the falling to earth.
Until time is lost, there is no need to wait.
The water relaxes
into pools.

3

Somewhere tension ends—
the flower that has pushed through soil and shadows
and the weight of sunlight
shatters into bloom; a pause beyond detail and measurement.
Above a star goes dark like one blade of grass crumpling,
its light finally touching the last eyes.
It fades from recognition
in a silence only the blind know
and perhaps no one understands.

I relax beneath a pine tree
in the soft fallen needles
and in the quiet of my eyes
I see only what surrounds me.

The Shaping of a Chapbook

an essay by Tamarie Spielman

Organizing a chapbook began for me with selecting about ten poems that I felt I could fit together to create a larger whole. They were not necessarily poems all about the same person or idea, but poems that touched in their ability to sometimes clarify, sometimes comment on each other. Looking back at this process I realize that I worked first from intuition. It is difficult to have distance from your own writing. Often I lose the details of my own poems when I have read them too many times. What I end up with is simply a strong "sense" of each poem. This sense I find almost impossible to explain. It is probably what made the poem in the first place, and to express the feeling in words again I think would take (or make) another poem. Using my sense of poems, I made the original selection of a group of poems.

Having narrowed down to particular pieces, I next thought about what I saw as unifying elements and individualizing elements in these writings. I wanted to order the poems so that they spoke to each other and so that the book took on a shape of its own. In this process, I kept coming back to a feeling that there is always a muse beneath my poems—some person, place, or experience that has affected me and that I may, *or may not,* be conscious of before writing. This idea became a centering element for me.

I chose "The Muse" to be the first poem, since it is both an introduction to the chapbook and to my writing. It points to the human and the magical as involved in making poetry. In tone, music, and voice the poem is an entrance to the poems that follow. It recognizes the conflict of feeling both part of a larger whole and feeling alone. After "The Muse" I put three personal voice poems, each dealing with this conflict in some way. One poem is written in my mother's voice; two are written in my voice addressed to different people.

As the fifth poem, I used an image poem to break up the narrative pieces. "6 Autumn Days" is a poem of change, close in place and feeling to many other voices in the book. I link it particularly with "The Hermit Sees Himself in the World Around Him." To me "6 Autumn Days" could be a collection of the hermit's observations, and it is full of "the sounds of stillness" that he hears. The poem uses its tone and progression of pictures, rather than statements, like the hermit, to communicate. I placed it before another series of narratives, including the hermit's, to draw attention to some of the nature scenes and images by first watching without explaining.

Beginning the second five poems of the chapbook I have another muse piece. "Sonnet for the Blend of Music and Nature" has an especially strong lyric and musical quality. Like "6 Autumn Days" it doesn't discuss; the sonnet communicates as much through sound as through words. The poem begins to consider the blending and breaking of humans and nature. While the narratives that preceded it focused on how humans interact with each other, those that follow the sonnet convey the tension between union with nature and solitude. For instance, "Strong Hold" reminds us of the "simple hold" on all our lives that nature has, while the hermit shows us the unique places within us where we are alone. "Tension," the last poem, accepts the reality of both being *with* and being *alone*. Poetry itself is a place where this happens—where communication is possible across the distances that separate us. Poetry is one of the magic meeting places, where for a moment, individuals join—the writer, the reader, and the world full of muses. The tension never really ends; its end in one poem is the beginning of another; for the poem too is the Muse.

Afterword

We planned this book as a journey, but now that you have completed it, you have only begun the much longer journey ahead of you. As Tam Spielman said, the end of one poem is the beginning of another. The end of this journey is the beginning of the next.

You do not need to *make* your life extraordinary; it already *is*. You need only look at the world through the eyes of a poet to see the extraordinary in the people around you and the experiences you have already had and will have.

Poetry begets poetry. "The poem, too, is the Muse," Tam says. Every assignment in this book gives examples to show you the way to poems of your own. You can easily follow this process in and out of this book, using poems you read and poems you write as muses to start new writing.

Strike out on your own paths and explore in any direction you can think of. Experience and language are so rich in possibilities for writing that you will never run out of good material.

Come back to this book and try assignments you skipped the first time through; or return to parts of the book that led you to your best poems; other good poems will be found there, perhaps even better ones.

Wherever your writing leads you, the journey is sure to bring you many discoveries about yourself and the world around you. May you fare well.

Index of Authors
and Titles